American Social and Political Thought

A Concise Introduction

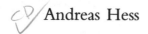Andreas Hess

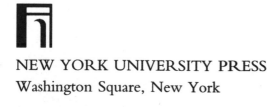

NEW YORK UNIVERSITY PRESS

Washington Square, New York

First published in the U.S.A. in 2000 by
New York University Press
Washington Square
New York, NY 10003

Typeset in Bembo
by Hewer Text Ltd, Edinburgh, and
printed and bound in Great Britain by
Creative Print and Design, Ebbw Vale, Wales

CIP data available from the Library of Congress
ISBN 0-8147-3629-7 (cloth)
ISBN 0-8147-3630-0 (paperback)

Contents

Preface

'I should be very much pleased if you could
find me something meaty on . . . California.'
(Karl Marx in a letter to Friedrich Sorge)

When Marx was writing to Friedrich Sorge more than a hundred years ago
he wanted to remind his comrade that he was waiting for substantial news
material from America. Against common belief and perception, Marx had a
declared interest in things American – politically, socially and intellectually.

In contrast, when confronting Europeans with American social and
political thought nowadays one is often faced with ignorance – an ignorance
that occasionally is even proud of its 'know-nothing' attitude. To some
people, usually to be found right across the political spectrum, the United
States seems to be nothing more than a society built on the genocide of its
native population, the enslavement, enforced transportation and wilful
exploitation of black people from Africa, the banalisation and popularisation
of true (mostly European) *Kultur*, not to mention a 'structural McCarthy-
ism' that spied on and persecuted everyone who stepped out of line. In the
eyes of these critics, America and its citizens are also ignorant when it comes
to geography, they are unaware of or do not care about the rest of the world
– an attitude that seems surprising partnered with the imperialist desire to
sell Hollywood products and McDonald's hamburgers to the world. To sum
it up, the United States is regarded as inimicial to any serious intellectual
enterprise.

It is quite remarkable that not only so many European, but also numerous
American intellectuals seem to be drawn to the popularisation and/or
confirmation of such perceptions. Even the most logical historical arguments are rejected: was it not the United States that saved Europe from
twentieth-century barbarism, despite the supposed superiority of European
Kultur and civilisation? Is it not the United States where intellectuals found
refuge from European intolerance, persecution and frequent anti-intellec-

tualism? And last but not least: is it not social and political thought that has found a safe haven in America and that has encountered an open society willing, since its very beginnings, to experiment with democratic ideas?

Yet if one studies the headlines and articles of newspapers and magazines that carry reports about the latest theoretical treatises from America (usually written by people from the cultural apparatus, that is, intellectuals), one is left with the impression that American public philosophy consists solely of self-congratulatory essayism or hyper-critical polemics. America is often viewed as producing only 'shots from the hip', that is no-substance – yet nevertheless celebrated – provocations from the Fukuyamas and Chomskys of this world. Yet against such a politically biased perception of the American intellectual tradition, and against a reductionist view of its politics and society, it must be stressed again and again that American social and political thought consists of much more; it is rich in its discussion of all possible aspects of democracy and it is far more differentiated, multilayered and sophisticated than the all too common anti-American perception the critics maintain.

It makes little sense to label thought processes and intellectual expressions as indigenous to one individual country, yet at the same time it remains true that it was in America especially that the enlightenment process was not confined to lofty intellectual circles but was applied practically and helped to put in place uniquely American political and social processes and institutions. A dialectic relationship developed: institutions that were created by intellectual design also had an impact and helped to shape the further formation of the American intellectual tradition. Today, more than 200 years after the American republic was founded, one can stand back and observe the development of such a genuine American tradition of social and political thought. Yet the very fact that there is a genuine American tradition of social and political thought does not mean that thoughts developed in America cannot be applied elsewhere. Social and political thought has always bounced back and forth between particularistic aspects of what is unique to certain social and political circumstances and universalistic aspects of what is common and can be applied to all circumstances. However, the point is that only by looking at particular circumstances is one in a position to suggest that something is universal, and only by discussing the universal aspects do the unique and the particular stand out.

Ideally then, this text should enable its readers to see exactly this relationship between the universal and the particular. In more concrete terms, this involves, in the first instance, gaining a better understanding of why and how certain ideas developed solely in America. This book will have realised one important objective if it manages to clarify what some of the most acknowledged American intellectuals had to say about their own society and its politics. It is, in other words, an attempt to understand American democracy by looking at how American intellectuals themselves tried to understand and explain it. In universal terms, however (and this is my second objective), it is hoped that this book will also enable the reader to imagine and understand social and political thought beyond the boundaries of the United States. Particularly after the 'tremendous events of 1989' (Wolf Lepenies) and the beginning of a new democratic epoch, American democracy can serve as an example of how to deal with the problems and challenges posed to modern democracy. After all, John Locke's observation that in the beginning all the world was America may indeed have been given a new meaning, only needing a stealthy twist of history to become fully realised.

This book deals with some of the most acknowledged contributors and contributions to the American tradition of social and political thought. Yet, in its approach it consciously looks at the tradition from the viewpoint of the present. It is thus neither an attempt to write intellectual history nor a contribution to the history of ideas; it is merely one hermeneutic attempt to understand and explain American thought. However, trying to write an introductory text on American social and political thought is like trying to cut a path through a jungle. Amongst the many possible paths and choices, one must necessarily select and reduce the complexity of the universe of American thought to (in the best sense) simple and logical storylines. Having said that, I hope that my overall 'story' (a story that unfolds in thematical blocks whose connections may at first sight seem to be somewhat laboured) will finally develop into a picture that is clear and informative. In this respect my hermeneutic attempt appears as a mosaic where in the end the many parts, or building blocks, form one impression. The mosaic, however, has two layers: the first, entitled 'Thinking the Political: The Main Modes and Traditions of American Social and Political Thought', deals mainly with the basic political foundations and building blocks of the American intellectual tradition: 'Exceptionalism', 'Political Theology', 'Republicanism', 'Liberalism' and 'Pragmatism'. It attempts to cover interpretations of the time that began just prior to the founding of the American Republic and lasted until the end of the Gilded Age and well into the twentieth century. This first part aims mainly at preparing the ground for the second part, entitled 'Theorising the Social: Modern Applications of American Social and Political Thought'. It is in this second part, consisting of the chapters 'Democracy and Power', 'Justice and Injustice', 'Pluralism and Multi-culturalism', 'Civil Society, Social Theory and the Task of Intellectuals' and 'Social and Political Thought at the Dawn of the Twenty-first Century', that we will discuss how differentiated American social and political thought has become in the course of the twentieth century.

I stated above that in my selection I necessarily had to make some tough choices – particularly when it came to the choice of who to leave out. I pursued such a path in order to strengthen those arguments that I consider absolutely essential and crucial to an understanding of American thought. (Coverage of all aspects might have offered a fuller picture – but could also prove confusing and overwhelming.) As a sort of compromise, I decided to include at least one classic in each field; I also looked at the discussion that followed such pioneering work, sometimes with the intent to revise or refute the classic thesis, at other times (depending on the material) not referring directly to those classic writings at all. Concerning the 'logic' of my reduction of complexity, readers are advised to look at the two sections at the end of the book. The list of thinkers includes all those authors whose work is discussed in the main text, and the annotated bibliography offers the reader a broader picture and gives an extended list of readings on each subject. It also indicates to the reader precisely what I have left out.

What follows are 'snapshots' of topics that played a major role in America's intellectual tradition. It is not the history of intellectuals. In respect of the latter it is useful to consider Richard Hofstadter's account. In his attempt to interpret the regular patterns in American intellectual history, Hofstadter combined a thematic approach with a chronological one. In his groundbreaking study of *Anti-Intellectualism in American Life* (which, it must be said, is in many ways also a study of intellectual life in America), he identified various types of American intellectual.[1] Starting with the Puritan clergy and the Founding Fathers – the former inclined toward a 'respect for mind and intensity of spirit', the latter to 'a workable body of ideas' – this early culture was replaced in the course of the nineteenth century by what Hofstadter calls a 'mugwump culture'. This culture consisted of an 'upper-class reform movement' and a 'dispossessed patrician class' that tried to preserve and cultivate the legacy of earlier generations, yet failed somehow to do so, not least because it could not really bridge the gap between a culture that was 'refined, dessicated, aloof, snobbish' and the culture of the common folk.[2] Furthermore, while the mugwump culture helped to create and maintain important cultural institutions, it failed to acknowledge some of the most exciting literary and democratic statements of the writers of the time. Hofstadter draws on the New York literary critic Philip Rahv when he writes that it is justifiable to speak of a split into a 'paleface' and a 'redskin' culture.[3] This division already hinted at things to come: 'a painful separation between the qualities of mind and the materials of experience'.[4] In other words, a gap developed that forced the intellectuals to take sides in the struggle for democracy (in the sense that democracy meant more than democracy for the enlightened few). In practical terms this had a serious impact on how intellectuals' identity was shaped. Hofstadter sees the end of the Gilded Age as a watershed in this respect: 'Up to about 1890, most American intellectuals were rooted in a leisured patrician class . . . After 1890 this was no longer true to the same degree. The problem of identity once again became a difficulty for intellectuals.'[5] Only after 1890 is it appropriate to speak of intellectuals as a class. According to Hofstadter this was also due to the rising importance of higher education. Only at the turn of the century had a genuine university system developed, a system that was open to more than a tiny elite. The 1930s and 1940s were also crucial in the further scheme of development. Whereas in the past America had looked to Europe for intellectual inspiration, the experience of Fascism, National Socialism and Stalinism led many of the European-focused intellectuals 'home': 'Intellectuals were seized by a passionate desire to look anew to the United States.'[6] In the course of the following decades one could observe a remarkable shift: intellectuals who, because of their disappointment with Europe and its ideas, realigned with American democracy. Yet this shift was not without its problems; knowledge and power once again became entwined. Yet, different from and compared to the past, this time knowledge and power had become differentiated functions in a more complex society in which the division of labour was paramount. The solution for the split between 'intellectuals' and 'mental technicians', sometimes also called 'clerisy' and 'avantgarde' or 'associates of power' and 'critics of power', could not be as easy as some of the self-styled 'alienated' critics maintained. For Hofstadter, the choice was not and is not between a clear 'either'/'or'. According to the historian, the twentieth century has taught intellectuals a lesson: 'before any writer or thinker can look upon himself as a potentially productive mind, he has already been born into a particular situation in life and endowed with a character and temperament that are only in limited respects malleable. This is the range that fate gives him, and he must work within it.'[7] From this we should not conclude that Hofstadter is a fatalist or a believer in structural determinism; rather Hofstadter stresses that 'what matters is the openness and generosity needed to comprehend the varieties of excellence that could be found even in a single and rather parochial society.'[8]

By referring to Hofstadter's study at such length, I would like to stress that – although the following is not a history of American intellectuals – for the overall majority of intellectuals and thinkers whose work is subject to my interpretation, Hofstadter's insights and different labels still apply. The same holds true for the various problems and conflicts that Hofstadter reveals.

What I am left with at the end of this preface is to let the reader know with whom and with whose position I identify. I first have to say that not having a *Weltanschauung*, a fixed world view, I resisted the temptation to write a final chapter in which I would 'deliver', in terms of coming up with my own synthesis. However, having said that, I should at least admit that I sympathise with the ideas of radical liberalism as they have been put forward and as they can be found in the works of Albert O. Hirschman, Stephen Holmes and Judith Shklar. I would like to emphasise, though, that there is much that radical liberals can learn from the older republican tradition and in this context I have no problems conceding that the demise of republican ideas has been greatly exaggerated. In terms of a broader understanding of modern twentieth-century history and the role that America and American thought has played in it, I am deeply indebted to Dan Diner's groundbreaking study *Das Jahrhundert verstehen (Understanding the Century)*.[9] This is not the place to recall all of the arguments presented in Diner's work; I would just like to stress that it offers a very different understanding of the century compared to what Eric Hobsbawm and others have said about the role that America played in an *Age of Extremes*.

I don't want to close this preface without thanking the people who have helped me to clarify my ideas and who have prevented me from falling into traps or ending up in intellectual culs de sac. All of them contributed to this text – sometimes without even knowing what the final outcome would be: Jeffrey C. Alexander (Los Angeles), Karl-Heinz Klein-Rusteberg (Essen) and William Outhwaite (Sussex). I would also like to thank two anonymous reviewers at Edinburgh University Press who commented on an earlier proposal for this text. I am especially grateful to the people of Mutriku (Gipuzkoa) – particularly Pello Andonegi and Idoia Arrizabalaga – with whom over the years I have had many discussions on America as interpreted by a West German, countered by their interpretation as people of the Basque Country with a broad vision of the larger Hispanic cultural environment.

Finally I would like to thank Diana J. Holubowicz, a native New Yorker, with whom every paragraph of this book has been discussed. It is to her that I dedicate this book.

Parts of this text (on Judith Shklar and the 'new black intellectuals') have appeared previously, although in a slightly different form:

- Das Recht, Rechte zu haben – Liberalismus der Angst: Judith Shklars Begründung der Politischen Philosophie, in: Forum Humanwissenschaften, *Frankfurter Rundschau*, 21.10.1998;
- Bach und James Brown, Sushi und fried catfish – 'Das Individuum ist eine Minderheit': Die New Black Intellectuals in den USA, in: Forum Humanwissenschaften, *Frankfurter Rundschau*, 13.5.1997;
- 'The Individual is a Minority' – The Thin Line between Universalism and Particularism, in: *Soundings*, Issue 11 Spring 1999, pp. 22–34.

Notes

1. Richard Hofstadter: *Anti-Intellectualism in American Life* (New York: Vintage Books 1962). I refer here particularly to the last chapter in his book (pp. 393–432).
2. All quotes are from p. 399f.
3. Ibid. p. 403.
4. Ibid. p. 404.
5. Ibid. p. 407.
6. Ibid. p. 413.
7. Ibid. p. 431.
8. Ibid. p. 432.
9. Dan Diner: *Das Jahrhundert verstehen* (Munich: Luchterhand 1999).

Part I

Thinking the Political:
The Main Modes and Traditions
of American Social and Political Thought

Chapter 1

American Exceptionalism

Human geography approaches: Crèvecoeurs *Letters from an American Farmer*, Turner's Frontier thesis and Mahan's vision of the influence of sea power ● The advantage of more comprehensive views: the sociological and political explanations of America's exceptionalist history ● Tocqueville's political sociology ● Lipset's explanations for the First New Nation – Arendt's distinction between 'the social' and 'the political', the French and the American Revolution ● Shklar's non-reductionist reflections on American exceptionalism

One of the earliest attempts to interpret the differences between the Old and the New World was made by Hector St John de Crèvecoeur in his *Letters from an American Farmer.*[1] In his *Letters* Crèvecoeur argued that Americans differed from Europeans in that they knew no feudal bonds, no aristocracy, no kings and no state church, and that they differed further in that in America plenty of land was available and farmers did not work for a feudal landlord but for themselves. Land was extensive enough and the soil rich enough to guarantee the farmers' self-sufficiency. Crèvecoeur also pointed out that America provided settlers with the opportunity to refashion their identity; whereas in Europe, where many had led lives of little value, America offered them the opportunity to re-invent themselves, meaning that they could now act upon a set of new principles, new ideas and new opinions. Particular forms of religion and government assisted this transformation: the role of sects provided the basis for religious tolerance, and local government permitted the settlers not only to become Americans but also provided a framework within which they could conduct their own affairs as Virginians, Pennsylvanians, and so on.

Crèvecoeur's thought reflected well the period about which he wrote; it reflected an America which still had an open border to the West – the Frontier. In gaining an understanding of America as it was in the eighteenth century, one must survey three distinctly different phases of settlement. The earliest, bound to the shores, followed by a migration into the newly civilised and developed countryside, and leading lastly to the woods and beyond – the open Frontier. It was Crèvecoeur who argued that, in order to understand America in historical terms, one had to look closely at the concept of the Frontier, as it created in essence the division between civilisation and wilderness.

Almost one hundred years later, Frederick Jackson Turner and Alfred Thayer Mahan, both historians and strategical thinkers, took up Crève-coeur's call, reflecting further on the course of history that America had taken since. Turner in particular was concerned with an all-embracing, comprehensive explanation that determined the peculiar course that American history took.[2] In a way, he followed Crèvecoeur in that he based his explanation on the Frontier thesis; but in particular, Turner gained distinction through distancing himself from interpretations, that saw American history rooted firmly in the earliest moments of America's eastern settlement. For Turner, it was not the Atlantic coast and New England but rather the interpretation of the development of the Great West that provided the key to an understanding of the peculiarities of American history. In his view, while the Frontier moved westward, it became less and less European and developed more and more into a unique American experience. In Turner's account, overcoming boundaries led to progress, which in turn led to radical political transformation. Additionally, through its very nature, the Frontier provided an environment in which individualism and democracy could flourish, as it was not bound by the ties of the federal government, thereby avoiding conflict and providing an opportunity to escape. In short, while the earlier eastern settlement gave birth to American democracy, the Frontier promoted the conservation and development of American democratic values and institutions. Logically then, Turner predicted that with the closing of the Frontier new conflicts of a mainly industrial nature would in fact arise – conflicts which could no longer be counterbalanced by values stemming from the Frontier experience. An adjustment was therefore necessary; American democracy now had to learn how to assimilate the element of possible conflict in a new industrial society which no longer offered the opportunity of escape.

In contrast to Turner, Mahan did not think that America's destiny had been abruptly halted with the closing of the Frontier.[3] In fact, with specific observations on the steady decline of British hegemony, which was based mainly on sea power, Turner recognised a real chance for America to stretch beyond its own boundaries, in that, if there was a future, it would be built on the basis of an America that was aware of its capacity to develop its sea power. For Mahan, America's geographical position as a continent encouraged such a future; it had two coasts, providing access to two oceans.

Additionally, it had access to the Caribbean Sea, and a large, navigable river – the Mississippi. The continent's physical formation was also advantageous in that the seaboard had a vast hinterland and there was easy access to the sea. Large commerce became a realistic option because of the vast number of people settled on the shores; furthermore, in comparison with other sea powers' engagement in commerce and industry, America also had the added advantages of not being inclined towards despotism (like Spain) and not being in control of a colonial empire (like Britain). America had no such ties to impede its development and expansion. Thus, with a democratic political system where the government was in line with the will of the people and with an additional interest in foreign trade, yet with no aspirations to occupy foreign territory, America's rise to sea power was inevitable. It was almost as if Mahan's argument was that, as the Frontier came to an end, another Frontier was born. This new Frontier was the sea, and it was a Frontier where America's exceptionalist past would find its future.[4]

Yet, despite their all-embracing focus, Crèvecoeur, Turner and Mahan's understanding and interpretation of American exceptionalist conditions remained far from being comprehensive. Their outlook can be criticised as having relied too much on the tools of human geography in examining man's struggle against nature; in its conclusion, human action was necessarily derived from, reduced to or determined by these natural conditions. Accordingly, all three thinkers' interpretations of exceptionalism may to some extent be viewed as being both pre-political and pre-sociological. Their interpretations were also rather weak when it came to the conceptualisation of democracy, republicanism, liberty and so on. The progression towards more sociologically and politically oriented accounts of exceptionalism can be found in the works of Alexis de Tocqueville, Seymour Martin Lipset and in more specific terms in the work of Hannah Arendt and Judith Shklar.

Alexis de Tocqueville, a French aristocrat, was the least likely candidate to write about democracy in America. As one would expect from a man with an aristocratic background, Tocqueville had been highly critical of the French Revolution. The experience of the loss of human life together with the terror and the dictatorship of the Committee on Public Safety, was too high a price to pay for a revolution whose only lasting 'achievement' had been the centralisation of the French nation-state.[5] In comparison, and as recorded, the American Revolution (1776–1783), which preceded the French Revolution (1789–1799), appeared to have had more purpose and result. Not only did the American Revolution manage to avoid extensive bloodshed and the terror, it also established a stable democratic system based on values such as liberty and political equality – something that the French Revolution (and, one may add, the Old World in general) had failed to do. In 1831 Tocqueville had a chance to experience America for himself and a few years later two volumes of his reflections on the American cause appeared as *Democracy in America*.[6]

Tocqueville was well aware that the establishment of a republic in the New World was something completely unprecedented. Yet, to say that something is unprecedented and exceptional, one needs to employ a comparative element. Tocqueville chose Europe, focusing on France and England in particular. In his argument Tocqueville even went a step further, stating that, if in fact it was true that democracy in America was so radically new and beyond traditional comprehension, it would be necessary to develop new conceptual tools to analyse its performance. The tool he promoted for the study of this new democracy was called political science. It is in this respect that Tocqueville differed from the approaches discussed under the label of 'human geography'. Democracy and the study of it could not be reduced to the natural environment; social and political action had to be studied in their own right.

When questioning precisely how, in terms of social and political arrangements, America differed from the Old World one must look at a key passage in *Democracy in America* where Tocqueville introduces the 'law of laws', that is the principle of the sovereignty of the people. By the sovereignty of the people he implies 'society acting by and for itself'. This notion of the sovereignty of the people stands in direct contrast to the European understanding and interpretation of sovereignty, particularly the British conception of the sovereignty of the parliament. In the British case, the government that holds the majority in parliament has free rein – even to the extent of infringement of the rights of individuals. The American framework is different; no government body is allowed to take away the natural and constitutionally guaranteed rights of its citizens. Central to this understanding is of course the idea of rights in general, and as Tocqueville stresses again and again, it needs institutional provisions to guarantee both the sovereignty of the people and the rights of individual citizens.

There was, and there still is of course, no institutional provision that can fully realise a principle such as the sovereignty of the people – unless people and government become identical, which is impossible in a large nation state. Yet, as Tocqueville points out, the federalist decentralised structure and the intentional separation of powers in the American political system is the nearest thing to the realisation of this principle. This is due to the fact that the American political system guarantees that at each stage of the political process the citizens may voice their opinion. Tocqueville hints here at the federalist 'bottom-up' structure: starting with the local community, followed by the county level, then the state, and finally the Union. The 'top-down' elements are carefully constructed in that the Union remains strong enough to act when necessary and when reasonable to do so (for example in the case of war), but would usually restrain itself from intervening in local affairs. The compromise between the two levels of the Union and the states, as agreed at the Philadelphia Convention, was realised and represented through the establishment of a bicameral Congress. While the Senate represents the states on equal par with two senators per state, the state's individual representation in the House of Representatives is determined by the size of population (determined by a census that has to be repeated every ten years). But not only is there a carefully constructed division of labour within the bicameral Congress, there is also a separation of powers, achieved by the division and collaboration of the executive, legislative and judiciary branches of government. Tocqueville stressed that what was particularly new, and where the American republic differed most from constitutional arrangements in Europe, was the guarantee of rights through the judicial system, a system of courts that would act on all levels of the federal system, with the Supreme Court having the final say.

Tocqueville explains at some length the sophisticated institutional arrangements of the American political system to his European readers; yet for most contemporary readers his main and lasting contribution was the analysis of a distinct American political culture. Tocqueville draws a sharp distinction between two different cultures that arose in the south and in the north of the United States. The South he regarded as the equivalent to the French aristocracy in that an elite had others do the work; whilst the North could not be more different, particularly New England, which he regarded as the cradle of American democracy, inhabited by hard-working and industrious people who relied not on the work of others or on landed wealth but on their own capacity for labour and trade. Tocqueville considers the northern settlers to have been fortunate that historical circumstances had been quite favourable to their enterprise: most of the immigrants had had early experiences with local government in Britain; also most of these early settlers were of middle-class background, well read and educated – not least through their Puritan upbringing and training. These factors plus an emphasis on morals, helped to establish a political culture on which democratic institutions could eventually be built and could thrive upon: a political culture which encouraged public spirit, respect for laws, common sense, the experience of self-government and conducting their own affairs free of state coercion. This together with the absence of any notion of superiority, the disregard for corruption, the absence of despotic government and state churches contributed to an overall sense that a new civil society and a new civic culture was emerging. The later institutionalisation only confirmed what earlier experiences had told the people of New England, namely that in their newly conceived civil society power did not necessarily contradict freedom. The insistence on political equality and rights, so it seemed, was the appropriate American response to the class-ridden system of the Old World.

It took another hundred years before Exceptionalism became a paradigm and part of the canon within the social sciences. This may be attributed to the work and efforts of one particular political sociologist, Seymour Martin Lipset. Lipset referred directly to Tocqueville in his *The First New Nation*, *Continental Divide* and *American Exceptionalism*.[7] Yet the references to his predecessor should not obscure the fact that Lipset's sociological and political tools were more sophisticated, as not only did Lipset stand firm on the shoulders of two academic disciplines (whereas Tocqueville was just about to discover the new political science), but it is also important to acknowledge that Lipset had benefited from the opportunity of having been able to observe the social and political developments of nineteenth- and twentieth-century America.

Lipset sways between three particular influences, that of Tocqueville, the critical Marxist tradition and Max Weber. To be sure, all three predecessors argued that America was exceptional, yet all had different explanations. For Tocqueville it was the idea of rights and political equality that shaped America's political system and culture; for Marx, America was exceptional because it was a purer society in that conditions for capitalism were not hampered by feudalist remnants; for Weber, on the other hand, America was purer in its Protestant work ethic, which then again led to a purer capitalist spirit. Lipset makes references to all three influences, yet he answers the challenges posed by the three with a different explanation altogether, not treating their ideas in isolation, but rather unifying the varying notions into one coherent approach.

Lipset questions how an identity is acquired when starting out as a new nation. The usual Weberian response to this question of identity could not be called into play as tradition and rational-legal authority need a long time to become accepted and prevail. According to Lipset, it was only through charismatic leadership, such as that of George Washington, that rational and legal authority could be established. Washington not only helped to establish the constitutional framework, but also managed to manoeuvre it through the first stormy years of the new American republic. Parties were formed largely through his influence and that of other charismatic leaders; in turn, these parties then helped to build a political consensus. It is also important to recognise that these charismatic figures and their respective parties played a crucial role in determining the future course of the American political economy. As for the stabilising efforts of the early republic, Lipset refers to another Weberian explanation – that of values; he stresses the importance of hard work, self-discipline and individual initiative, all derived from the Protestant work ethic.[8] These values were not only promoted by the Protestant churches and sects but also by the intellectuals of the day. In this context, Lipset hints at another exceptionalist phenomenon: that, at least in the early years of the American republic, intellectuals and power were not separated; quite distinctively from Europe, American intellectuals combined scholarship with action. Also, from the early days onwards, American intellectuals had defended the ideas of democracy and political equality, as did the rest of the citizenry – conservatives and loyalists who were opposed to independence and the founding of the new republic emigrated (most of them to Canada); the ones who were conservative only in their values used the existing means of civic associations, such as churches, to voice discontent. Thus a truly conservative party could not emerge. Lipset's explanation of exceptionalist conditions also deals with historical materialists' arguments that no value system alone could explain the stability of the American republic – particularly not when one considers the record levels of inequality and poverty in twentieth-century America. There had to be direct political and social gains for the American working class. Ideologically and practically, inequality had to be kept at bay. Lipset explains the enormous capacity to keep conflict at bay through two explanations, one more 'political', the other more 'social'. The 'political' explanation is simple: in Europe the working class and its political organisations (including socialist or social-democratic parties) had to fight not only for social causes but also for political reform. It was very different in America where, since formal democracy was already in place, the working class was just another lobbying group amongst many others. The American working class did not have to fight for political reform, as that had already been achieved by the Revolution and the War of Independence. The 'social' explanation is that American society did not demand absolute social equality as Europeans did. Rather, the Americans focused on equality of achievement, which of course was aided by the presence of political equality. It was the possibility of equal access to education, guaranteed through political citizenship, which helped to keep the dream of achievement and equality alive. And again, one must understand equality and achievement as deeply American values: the emphasis on equality derived from the Revolution against the Old World; the focus on achievement stemming from the Protestant work ethic.[9] For

Lipset it is this peculiar relationship between equality and achievement that explains the remarkable continuity and stability of American society. It must be noted however that these factors do not inhibit change, but recognise change as an adjustment to the system – not as a complete break from it. With such an explanation, Lipset clearly follows the groundwork of Tocqueville, but moves beyond lay-terms and expresses his theories in 'proper' sociological and political terms, such as the value system in context of the material setting or as the relationship between conflict and consensus – the latter providing the background to the former.

Lipset's sociological and political conceptualisations were paralleled by other more philosophically grounded interpretations of American exceptionalism or distinctiveness. Two distinguished political philosophers stand out in particular, Hannah Arendt and Judith Shklar. In her writings on America Hannah Arendt referred time and time again to Tocqueville's observation of the insistence on political rights and political equality; yet her interpretations of exceptionalist America were shaped by contemporary concerns, such as her own experiences of totalitarianism. Hannah Arendt was trained as a philosopher and was a Jewish intellectual who had been lucky enough to escape National Socialism. These experiences, together with a Europe in ruins, a Europe that was finally liberated by the Americans, led her to rethink some of the major concepts of political thought, particularly in light of her later experiences in the United States. Thinking about 'the political', as opposed to 'the social', and identifying 'the political' with the American political experience and 'the social' with the French Revolution, Arendt had a particularly strong sense of why the American experience had been so exceptional. For Arendt, it had always been somewhat anomalous that the French experience of revolution had become the universal reference point, particularly when seen in light of later events, such as the Russian Revolution. The American experience however, continued to be neglected – at least in terms of universal respect and reference. In her book *On Revolution* Arendt argues that it should rather be the exceptional experience of America that should serve as a guide; it is, after all, a country that has known no dictatorship or totalitarian regime.[10]

Arendt's main argument is based on a dichotomy in that the French Revolution received its world-wide recognition due mainly to the fact that its main feature was that it was dominated and led by social questions, that is social inequality and class distinctions. The demands for social equality provided the answer to a feudalist past and inherited class membership. In Arendt's interpretation, the preoccupation with 'the social' led people to think in terms of historical necessities – not least resulting from the assumption that it was nature itself that demanded social equality. Here Arendt sees a continuity of reasoning, first from Rousseau to Hegel, then from Hegel to Marx and finally from Marx to the Russian Revolution. The terror of the French Revolution (and later the Russian Revolution) can mainly be explained by this kind of reasoning. In this respect the bourgeois and the proletariat were just acting out what the natural course of history demanded from them. In Arendt's opinion, intellectuals and philosophers played a major role in interpreting what was natural and what history demanded. Yet, as Arendt remarks critically, in playing this interpreter role, the *hommes de lettres* ironically also became detached from the people.

The situation was altogether different in America. Free from inherited social inequality, America considered its situation as a new beginning where its citizens could promote and develop the idea of political freedom, where class and inequality were only remnants of a distant European past. Accordingly, American rhetoric avoided the terminology of historical necessities and the rhetoric of class and used instead the rhetoric of rights. The citizen, not the bourgeois, was its major player. As a consequence, where the French Revolution had ended in Napoleonic dictatorship and where the French, up to the present day, had experienced five republics, the American Revolution and the War of Independence had not only avoided terror and major bloodshed, but had led to the constitution of a republic which lasted and remains stable to the present day. Arendt also stresses that the Americans were fortunate to have had intellectuals amongst their ranks who did not see themselves as superior to other citizens but who rather had become citizen philosophers, occupied solely with the question of how to conceive and stabilise political freedom and equality. To summarise Arendt's arguments: while the French had thought about 'the social', the Americans had thought about 'the political'. While the first notion is bound up with determining what is historically necessary to achieve social equality (and consequently it became entrapped in the same logic), the second notion is bound to freedom and the achievement of political equality. Other Western nations also eventually developed into democracies, yet it was a different story altogether in that 'the social' determined 'the political' – unlike America where it was 'the political' which turned out to be decisive.

As with Hannah Arendt, Judith Shklar had not been born an American citizen. Like Arendt, Shklar had left Europe to find exile, first in Canada, before finally settling in the United States. And again, as in the case of Arendt, persecution in Europe, the experience of emigration and of the relatively safe haven that America had become for refugees led Shklar to an appreciation of American political forms. Yet, to list Judith Shklar among exceptionalist thinkers is certainly problematic since she more than once took issue with the exceptionalists, whom she regarded as reductionists in that they gave monolithic answers to the complex questions that American politics and society posed. Nevertheless, in her discussion of Hannah Arendt's work and in her own evaluations of the Founding Fathers' contribution, she acknowledged the unique circumstances under which the American republic took shape.[11] Shklar agreed with most of what Arendt had to say: the unprecedented social and political conditions under which the American Republic was first conceived, the success the Founding Fathers had in absorbing the revolutionary spirit and energy and preserving its political institutions, and the relative success and achievements of the American Revolution when compared to the problems that resulted from the French Revolution. Yet Shklar also pointed towards the weaknesses in Hannah Arendt's interpretation: the Founding Fathers managed to ignore the 'social question' and to focus instead on political rights and political freedom only because America at the time was relatively free of misery; the Americans did not turn into professional revolutionaries as newly conceived institutions, such as the Constitution, were flexible enough to respond to the needs of the citizenry.[12] Shklar also hints at what was completely absent in Arendt's account – namely that the American Republic had to fight a Civil War in order to secure the earlier promises of the Constitution, particularly when it came to the question of citizenship. Arendt also appeared weak when it came to contemporary issues; according to Shklar, she had no knowledge of post-Civil-War history, Southern politics and the more contemporary constitutional issues which dealt with citizenship.

Where Shklar differed from Arendt was in her particular interpretation of the environment of newness that the Americans found themselves in. It was not that she disagreed completely with Arendt's general statements, it was more that she discovered two peculiar lines of arguments within the Founding Fathers that are not discussed in Arendt's work. One view, called the 'party of hope', represented in Thomas Paine and Thomas Jefferson, referred to the rejection of and radical rupture with everything that related to European history. Paine and Jefferson not only firmly insisted on living in the present, but this attitude also allowed them to nurture bright hopes for the future. In opposition to this view was what Shklar terms the 'party of memory', as represented by John Adams and to a certain extent James Madison. Both Adams and Madison suggested taking a closer look at the past in order to find out exactly what had gone wrong with classic European republicanism. This view was much more pessimistic in its outlook; in essence, it was what led this faction of the Founding Fathers to construct certain built-in security mechanisms within the Constitution. As Shklar has pointed out, both views and the public discussion of both shaped the First

New Nation. There is thus not one monolithic way of coming to terms with a new beginning. To be sure, this reminder throws a different, more sophisticated light on the reality of exceptionalist American democracy. Additionally, Shklar's argument warns us not to treat any complex social and political mechanism such as American society and politics under one label only – and if the rhetoric of American exceptionalism should prevail, it can only do so when discussed in relation to all aspects of American society and politics.

Notes

1. Hector St John de Crèvecoeur's *Letters from an American Farmer* was first published in 1782. Various editions of the text have appeared since then. I refer here to the edition that was published in London: Penguin 1997.
2. Frederick Jackson Turner's *The Frontier in American History* first appeared in 1920. Numerous other editions have appeared since then. I refer here to the edition that was published in New York: Dover Publications 1996.
3. Alfred Thayer Mahan's *The Influence of Sea Power on Modern History* first appeared in 1890. I refer here to an edition of the text published in New York: Dover Publications 1996.
4. It could well be argued that a prolongation of the concept of the Frontier took place through developing naval power into air power and finally from air power into space.
5. Tocqueville reflected on the French Revolution in his *L'Ancien Régime et la Révolution* (1856).
6. Alexis de Tocqueville: *Democracy in America* first appeared in 1835 and 1840. I refer here to the edition that was edited by J. P. Mayer (London/New York: Fontana Press 1994).
7. *The First New Nation* (New York: Basic Books 1962); *Continental Divide* (New York/London: Routledge 1990); *American Exceptionalism* (New York: Norton 1996).
8. It was indeed the German sociologist Max Weber who first thought about the Protestant work ethic. The only reason why Max Weber is not dealt with in this chapter is that his writings do not amount to what I would call a fully developed exceptionalist position. For his writings on America and the role that religion plays in American life, see the next chapter.
9. Werner Sombart, a German sociologist who visited the United States, stressed the same point in his study *Why Is there No Socialism in the United States?* (first published in 1906; an English translation appeared in London: Macmillan 1976). A variation on the theme provoked an article by the American political scientist Andrei S. Markovits: 'Why Is There No Soccer in the United States?' in: *Leviathan* 4/1987, pp. 486–525.
10. *On Revolution* (New York: Viking Press 1963).

11. *Redeeming American Political Thought* (Chicago: Chicago University Press 1998) and *Political Thought and Political Thinkers* (Chicago: Chicago University Press 1998).

12. At the same time Shklar acknowledges that the Founding Fathers were also the inventors of American political science, a thesis that somewhat resembles Tocqueville's idea that new conditions led to the foundation of a new political science.

Chapter 2

Political Theology

The religious roots of American social and political thought ● The Puritan settlers and the tradition of dissent ● Real and perceived: Exodus and New Jerusalem ● Tocqueville's analysis of the relationship between religious belief and political democracy ● Weber's emphasis on the role of Protestant sects for the formation of the American middle class ● Shklar's emphasis of the thin line between sacred ideas and secularised political practice: understanding the co-existence of theological ideas, social contract theory and historical events ● Miller's rejection of human geography explanations and his inter- pretation of the development of the New England mind ● Bercovitch's radicalisation of Miller: the creation of the American Jeremiad through rituals of socialisation

The German legal theorist Carl Schmitt once remarked that all modern political ideas have religious origins and must therefore be understood as quasi-secularised concepts. The history of American social and political thought is no exception to this rule; as a matter of fact, the American case in particular probably demonstrates the general rule better than any other. When the Puritans first set foot on American soil, they did so conscious of the fact that they were bound to build the New Jerusalem. They saw themselves as part of the Exodus as the Bible told it and, as one can imagine, the newly found land seemed to reinforce the biblical narrative. Yet, apart from what the Protestant settlers believed in, it is also important to acknowledge what had triggered their emigration in the first place. For their views (of which the Exodus was just a part) the settlers had been regarded as dissenters in their home country, and being dissenters from the Church of England they had had to leave England. The dissenters who constituted the first wave of immigration into America were usually well-read and keen on education; additionally, they had some experience of governing their own affairs – and this knowledge would necessarily increase while conducting their own affairs on American soil. The Puritans also did not want to relive and promote the religious intolerance (and in some cases persecution) that they had left behind in Europe.

Over the years, various communities were established. Not all were of Puritan origin, and certainly in the beginning not all the settlers were convinced democrats. Yet over time the different religious groups learnt how to respect each other – first in the form of territorial claims and then increasingly as different groups that were not limited to one territory or to a particular stretch of land. Pluralism, that is the existence and acknowledgement of different religious groups, became increasingly accepted. It would be misleading to imagine this pluralism as the pluralism that we know today; after all, the early forms of Protestant dissent could turn out to be quite dogmatic, particularly when one was taking the idea of delivering missions or pronouncing prophecies as seriously as the first generations of settlers did. Yet, in the end, there were simply too many different groups and factions of Protestant belief, hence there was no serious alternative to the acceptance of pluralism.

The acceptance of pluralism and religious freedom would later be acknowledged, particularly in the First Amendment of the Constitution (1787/carried into effect 1789). The First Amendment prohibits the establishment of the equivalent to the Church of England or of any other 'official religion' (as was the case with Catholicism in nineteenth- and early twentieth-century France, Spain and Italy). Interestingly enough, the First Amendment, which established that 'Congress shall make no law respecting an establishment of religion, or prohibiting the free exercise thereof', continues with the freedom of speech, freedom of the press and 'assures the right of the people peaceably to assemble'.[1] This shows that pluralism and religious freedom went hand in hand with other fundamental democratic rights. Yet what appears together in the one short paragraph of the First Amendment had a longer social and political history, and codified a general link between religion and democracy which needs to be examined more thoroughly.

It was Alexis de Tocqueville who first discussed the relationship between religious belief and American democracy.[2] One must add here that at the time Tocqueville visited the United States, Catholicism had already firmly taken root – particularly through mass immigration from Ireland. Thus, his comments must be seen not only as confirming religious pluralism among various Protestant factions, but also as a pluralism that included Catholicism. Having said that, Tocqueville never forgets to emphasise the particular relevance of the earlier Protestant settlers. This earlier influence is acknowledged in the author's statement that in America politics and religion had agreed from the start. The link that binds the two realms together socially is mores, morality. The Protestant sects may be following their own split agenda, yet they are all part of Christendom, which teaches moral behaviour. According to Tocqueville, the experience of freedom only enforces this Christian belief and, while in the realm of politics there is tension, in their social life Christian citizens can gain a sense of order and peace from moral religious education. It was this relationship and lived experience that led to the respect and acknowledgement of the American revolutionaries and framers of the Constitution.[3] Tocqueville reflects on this and stresses that religious mores as practised in civil society helped to establish and guarantee the new republic framework. For him, there is a mutually beneficial effect, a link between the ideas of Christianity and liberty.[4] Thus, in America religion and enlightenment were not in opposition – as was the case in the French Enlightenment; rather, they co-existed and thrived off each other. Mores helped to minimise the idea that everything had to be organised and had to be guided by laws. Having self-guiding mores takes a lot of pressure away from the process of law-making. What Tocqueville discovered was nothing less than the kernel and inner secret of American civil society – this was after all a society that could function well without relying entirely on a central state or a federal government. Additionally, moral life that stemmed from religious belief also had other benefits: it refrained from and controlled some of the excesses that come with seeking status and equality. As Tocqueville again reveals, it may not completely prevent people from gaining what they seek, but at least it ensures that 'people use only honest means to enrich themselves'.[5]

It was the German sociologist Max Weber who, at a later point, elaborated on Tocqueville's observations and distinctions. Like Tocqueville, Weber had visited the United States (in 1904); but while the French aristocrat experienced the expansion of American democracy under Andrew Jackson, Max Weber saw a capitalist America that was in full swing. For Weber, Protestant ideas served as a major force in the creation of capitalism. The Calvinists' belief in leading an ascetic life, working hard and rejecting worldly pleasures particularly helped them to save and accumulate capital and to invest profits in capitalist enterprises. But this was only in the grand scheme of things; in particular, Weber was interested in the role Protestant sects and voluntary associations played in civil society in America.[6] It is here that he differed from Tocqueville. While Tocqueville saw the different religious sects mainly as a stabilising and supportive factor in American civil society and democracy (and as a restraining force when it came to money-making), Weber had an interest in how religious voluntary associations and the Protestant spirit directly helped in developing capitalism and the entrepreneurial spirit in America. That which Weber saw as so distinctive in the United States had been the clear and formal separation of religion and state – hence no state church, but rather the existence of a number of sects, mostly of Protestant origin. When compared to religious forms in Europe, two distinct organising principles could be identified in the United States. First, while affiliation with a European state church is obligatory and comes almost 'naturally' through family ties, the American sect was a voluntary association, based not on dogma and life-long membership but on individual decision. Second, what Weber saw as different was the fact that while members of the European state church gathered people from all walks of the stratified society at large the Protestant sects in America in contrast were of mainly middle-class origin. Being a member of the local Methodist or Baptist church was advantageous for these middle-class individuals: if one was to be accepted by the local congregation, it could be a door-opener to the local community at large. In the best case, it could mean credit-worthiness and, as a result, upward mobility and success. For Weber, the very fact that one's ascendancy into the middle class, or even higher entrepreneurial circles, depended on the intermediary forms of civil society (in this case Protestant sects) tells us something about American society in general; accordingly, America could not be understood, unless one understood the role of voluntary associations. As Weber points out, the experience of active membership in the local church served as a kind of training ground for things to come: 'full citizenship status in the church congregation was the precondition for full citizenship in the state'.[7]

Up to this point the focus of discussion has been more on the formal aspects of the link between particular religious forms of belief and American democracy; not much has been said about the specific content of these religious forms and what impact they may have had on formulating political ideas. In one of her essays published in the collection with the revealing title *Redeeming American Political Thought* Judith N. Shklar discusses some of these implications.[8] She argues that in order to fully understand the idea of the 'model republic' and the American mission in the works of Thomas Paine, Thomas Jefferson and the democratic ideas of the Jacksonian Age, one must refer back to the Puritans. Shklar describes the Puritans' democracy as one that was 'both exclusive and authoritarian'.[9] To hold a position in the community one had to have true qualities, a calling; but a true quality such as merit could not be inherited; rather the individual concerned must have demonstrated those qualities and capabilities.

It was of course the task of the clergy to single out the candidates for office. In response, the selected candidates had to show responsibility; they had to demonstrate that they did what the majority of the community wanted them to do. Yet the clergy not only exercised power in this 'test-run for democracy', they also influenced the formation of political ideas by delivering political sermons, which of course were loaded with biblical interpretations, particularly from the Old Testament.

An early interpretation of 'we the people' had to include a reference to the chosen people of Israel. This notion was promoted through a unique constellation: the parallel that could be drawn from settlers crossing the Atlantic and establishing new communities, as in the Old Testament stories. In short, the time was interpreted in prophetic modes and was delivered in the language of providence, revivals and/or re-awakenings. People had not lived up to the Word, they had fallen from grace, yet they would try again by re-affirming and re-assuring the common goal of salvation. It is also important to stress – particularly when one understands the later manifest destiny – that the 'errand into the wilderness' (an expression that Shklar takes from Perry Miller), saw himself as a model for the rest of the world. Taking all of this into consideration, one must question how it then became possible to link this political theology to the more secularly defined idea of the social contract, as suggested by John Locke. The answer is simple: through concrete historical circumstances. As Shklar explains, the Puritans had an agreement not only with God but also among themselves (in order to fulfil collectively the tasks of God); additionally, the communal responsibility to fulfil Israel's mission made them resistant to tyranny. Thus they were 'quite prepared to accept a secular explanation of their difficulties with England as well as a purely political justification for resistance . . . Locke was simply added on to a religious doctrine of government.'[10] Shklar explains further: 'The great Mr Locke had simply explained to them in immediate terms what they already understood from contemplating the story of Noah. His prescriptions were perfectly compatible with their own sense of their situation.'[11] In the light of this constellation of political theology, social contract theory and historical events, it is simple to understand why the British king and his American representatives were seen as acting against both the law of man and the law of God. It also explains why rights (as interpreted through Lockean terms) became popular: only by referring to inalienable rights were Americans in a position to cut the ties with England. As Shklar suggests: 'For the people of Israel had not fallen into anarchy, after all. It had found new and virtuous judges in its towns and villages, and above all the Continental Congress meeting in Philadelphia was composed of good men . . . The king was indeed a tyrant and a just war against him was called for, but all this would act as a scourge and Israel would emerge cleansed from the ordeal. It would come out of a corruption and decline like Rome's and the Babylonian captivity and would be restored to continue its mission.'[12]

In the writings of Tom Paine, particularly his *Common Sense*, the language that had so far been of the mixed parentage of religion and natural rights eventually pursued a more secular path without giving up completely missionary ideas. In Paine's political writings there was no longer a clergy or a religious elite to deliver the sermons of independence and providence. The same things were now the task of every citizen; more than that, the American struggle turned out to be the first struggle in an attempt to save the world. In the words of Shklar, who describes this turn from particularistic circumstances to universalistic values, 'A struggle for freedom is inherently important for everyone who hopes anywhere . . . All men, not just the children of Israel, were now fit for government.'[13] Thus, Paine's understanding of new citizenship was inclusive rather than exclusive (as was the Puritans' understanding of membership in the congregation): 'Anyone who wanted to be a democratic citizen belonged to the people.'[14]

To be sure, Thomas Paine was not an agnostic but rather a Deist; this meant that the idea of a 'true religion' would never be absent from his writings. Religious thought thus became desacralised and hidden in secularised rhetoric. Thomas Jefferson, an admirer of Paine, is an exemplar of this type of writing, particularly in his work about the new, unbound American democracy, where traits of a hidden political theology can be found. For him (as for Paine) 'the world belonged entirely to the living' and 'it was inherent in democracy that the present alone should matter'.[15] As Shklar stresses, Jefferson thought it appropriate to have a revolution every twenty years, including a change of the Constitution and the relevant institutions in order to avoid social sclerosis. To achieve such a flexible state, the hemisphere had to stay as open as possible and thus there should be no boundaries to Americans. The American polity was thus conceived of as being unlimited in principle and, as Shklar stresses, that contradicted the classic notions of membership in a democracy that had always depended on boundaries and a properly defined polity. Here for the first time was a democracy where these boundaries were not clear and where membership also knew no limits. It became obvious: through Jefferson, the prophecy inherent in the rhetoric of political theology had become part of the principally unlimited American agenda.

The implications of this metamorphosis are still to be felt in the twentieth century and are as valid today as they were in the nineteenth century – and this is by no means limited to the realm of politics and political ideas. Just how deeply this metamorphosis has penetrated the consciousness of American citizens is the subject of the historical analysis of Perry Miller and the work of Sacvan Bercovitch. While Miller's work is more historical, Bercovitch's deserves credit for having reflected upon and spelled out the lasting implications of Miller's historical analysis.

Undoubtedly the Harvard historian Perry Miller must be acknowledged as having made the pioneering attempt at comprehending the transition of mind from the earliest Puritan communities to the more secularised creed of New England. Two books in particular are of importance, *The New England Mind – From Colony to Province* and a collection of essays entitled *Errand into the Wilderness*.[16]

The New England Mind is a historical analysis of 'the architecture of the intellect brought to America by the founders of New England'.[17] Miller's hypothesis is that, whereas in the beginning constant intellectual reference was made to Europe, in the long run the Puritans also had to come to terms with and make sense of the new environment they found themselves in. In other words, while in the beginning we see a life of the mind which is 'static, architectonic, and formal', in short, European, over the course of two centuries we can observe an increasing tendency to deal with problems that were specifically American – and therefore 'not on the schedule'.[18] While the first generation had no problem in practising and living according to their religious belief – it was meant to serve as an ideal example and have a function in Europe – the following generations had to cope with the problem that what they had to say about their American experience was no longer of any interest to the Old World. Europe had witnessed not only the Great Revolution and Restoration but also the spread of the Reformation on the Continent, which included the participation of all Protestant religious factions. Why should Europeans learn from America and the construction of 'the city upon the hill' when the European house was refurbished anyway?

Miller's analysis starts with a telling example of how early religious pursuits can turn into rituals. For the early Puritans the celebration of Thanksgiving was crucial. But the celebration itself could only take place after the harvest was done – and the date would of course vary according to the circumstances. The change of Thanksgiving to a more specific day and time (the fourth Thursday of the month of November) symbolises better than anything else the success of society; it no longer celebrated God's work but rather society's own successful labour. As Perry Miller rightly concludes, the religious overtones had given way to the celebration of human toil and 'when this happens, Calvinism is dead'.[19] We might add here that this is also the marking point where European colonists become Americans – at least in terms of the life of the mind.

To be sure, it took a long time before such radical change could occur and in the meantime there were a lot of opportunities to not rejoice, but rather to feel humiliated because of the lack of success. The question also arose of exactly how one could determine, after one had given up the idea of being an experiment for Europe, how far one had developed or degenerated? The answer still had to be a religious one and to reflect about the state of things the Jeremiad was 'invented'. The Jeremiad was a sermon, a 'subtle exploration of the labyrinth of sin and regeneration',[20] usually delivered with the purpose of gathering and binding the community together. It must be noted here that on first sight this sermon relied heavily on the books of the Old Testament, Isaiah and Jeremiah in particular, but the Jeremiad also served a practical purpose in setting a goal. Thus the Jeremiad not only fulfilled the function of properly spelling out what was so unique about the exceptional American circumstances but it also 'manufactured a vision' (P. Miller).

As Miller further highlights, with increasing trade and the beginning of westward expansion new circumstances arose which had to be integrated into the religious view and vision. What the historian actually demonstrates by looking at the increasingly standardised Jeremiads is the metamorphosis from a colony that was originally built on religion into a province where mercantile trade and the economic realm became central but were still legitimated by belief. What the Jeremiad does is to function as a ritual of confession, which allowed Americans to find stability amidst change; it shows 'how intelligence copes with . . . a change it simultaneously desires and abhors'.[21] But the Jeremiad also had another advantage; not only did it help Americans to come to terms with mercantile capitalism, it also helped to accommodate the social tension stemming from those new economic activities. In that respect the Jeremiad also functioned as a silencer with the cohesive effect of preventing the emerging society from falling apart. Yet in order to have this controlling and cohesive effect, the churches also had to open themselves to all inhabitants of the town. Access to the congregation had to be made easier. Church meetings had to take place in public and were forced to become more voluntary in character. Miller describes this process of opening and openness as the birth of 'federal theology' – 'federal' meaning that the communities now consisted not purely of a closed community of convinced 'saints' but rather of a new plural, federal form with a theoretical centre, half-way members of the congregation, and the outer 'ring' of members who lived in the town yet had no great confessional 'history'. It was this change, which Miller describes as a change from the 'private' religion to the 'communal chant', that provided a major breakthrough in terms of participatory experiences – something which, as it turned out, was to become a precursor to future pluralism and federalism. While *The New England Mind* is the intellectual history of this major transformation, *Errand into the Wilderness* explores more the possible 'themes' that stem from this change. In conceptualising the exceptionalist character of America in the terms of political theology Miller clearly rejects the 'human–geography' approach of Frederick Jackson Turner and others; in his view, the Frontier thesis does not permit insight into the dynamic aspects of American culture. It is different with concepts and metaphors stemming from political theology, such as 'the errand'. Placed in the context of 'wilderness', the explanatory outcome is certainly more plausible than the Frontier thesis.

Miller begins by explaining the two definitions of the word errand. It could mean, first, a short journey by an inferior person sent out with the purpose of performing a service; or, second, it could refer to the fulfilment of a purpose itself. According to Miller's application of the two definitions in the context of the New England frame of mind, they actually represent two phases:

1. The period of the early settlement when the Puritans thought of themselves as inferiors sent out to America to explore the potential for a new life under God, and to report back to Europe.

2. The period when the settlers realised that there was no longer the need to report back to Europe; their effort had been rendered purposeless by the changes in Europe.

Having been deserted by their 'master' (Europe), they had to create a purpose – and they did so in the theological language available to them. The result was the errand, the Jeremiah who became a purpose in himself. Needless to say, this biblical figure ran into all kinds of problems when confronting the real world. Perry Miller has summarised the dilemmas in the most colourful of words:

'The exhortation to a reformation which never materialises serves as a token payment upon the obligation, and so liberates the debtors. Changes there had to be: adaptations to environment, expansion of the frontier, mansions constructed, commercial values undertaken. These activities were not specifically nominated . . . They were thrust upon the society by American experience; because they were not only the works of necessity but of excitement, they proved irresistible – whether making money, haunting taverns, or committing fornication. Land speculation meant not only wealth but also dispersion of the people . . . The covenant doctrine preached . . . had been formulated in England, where land was not to be had for the taking; its adherents had been utterly oblivious of what the fact of a frontier would do for an imported order, let alone for a European mentality. Hence I suggest that under the guise of this mounting wail of sinfulness, this incessant and never successful cry for repentance, the Puritans launched themselves upon the process of Americanisation.'[22]

What Miller stresses here is that political theology is not without tensions.

Being theology, fulfilment never comes; yet at the same time this theology served a cohesive purpose: it calmed the social and political tensions by keeping the dream alive.

In his *American Jeremiad* Sacvan Bercovitch goes a step further. He radicalises Miller in that he liberates the Jeremiad from the early religious and historical context and positions it as a rhetorical device which succeeded in establishing and renewing the American dream for more than 200 years. Yet this 'liberation' is not a complete one: Bercovitch's interpretation still refers back to political theology in that the Puritan rhetoric is regarded as *the* major influence in shaping political beliefs; the revisionist's meaning of the Jeremiad only becomes a broader one in that the figure of the Jeremiad is now seen as shaping the *entire* social and cultural perception of Americans today.

Of particular interest is the middle-range approach that Bercovitch chooses to follow; he neither says that there is one straightforward line from the Puritan origins and their belief to the present-day America, nor does he get lost in arguments about historical detail and singularity. As he explains, he 'sought to establish connections between rhetoric and history'.[23] He assumes that there is indeed an organic strand in American history, even though it started out as a mainly agrarian society to become a fully industrialised society, passing through periods of urbanisation, a transportation revolution, the transformation of the political economy, and even a civil war. At each of these stages or periods, America managed to both change and maintain its identity. For Bercovitch, this was only possible as a result of 'rituals of socialisation', which led to the formation of an ideological consensus. Such a cultural hegemony, based on political sermon, was established early. Yet being theological in nature the content of the sermon could never be proven. It was universal but at the same time unachievable. This does not mean that it had no material or cultural effects, it just meant that it was part of the 'logic' never to reach the final aim; in other words: the path became the aim. One must question how this was possible.

How exactly could one interpret the holy text in the complex context of being both a colony (and thus a part of the British Empire) and then becoming an independent republic? Here Bercovitch refers directly to what Perry Miller had called 'the errand in the wilderness': an errand could 'venture on another's behalf or . . . venture of one's own'. He argues further that 'the Puritans' tragedy was that their errand shifted from one meaning to another in the course of the seventeenth century.'[24] First the Puritans had hoped for an England that could be reformed from the periphery, but later they had to derive meaning from their unique experiences in America. The sermon of the Jeremiad of the Old World addressed the state the world was in; to be sure, there was not much hope. How could there be in a static order? In the New World, in contrast, the sermon took on a slightly different meaning; after all, inherited class distinctions did not play a role. As a result, the missionary interpretation became increasingly stronger; there was hope after all. Whereas in the Old World, God would punish, in the New World's experience his voice became corrective. Hardship turned into promise. The mission of the Jeremiad was thus born, not least due to the fact that an element of social reality corresponded to it.

Bercovitch dissents from Miller in that he does not subscribe to his predecessor's Frontier thesis, that is that the errand needed the wilderness and the Frontier. For Bercovitch the American Jeremiad did not stop preaching with the end of the Frontier; rather it extended into the twentieth century until the present day. Despite borders and boundaries, the American mission continued. America 'could read its destiny in its landscape'; it had 'a population that, despite its bewildering mixture of race and creed, could believe in something called an American mission, and could invest that patent fiction with all the emotional, spiritual, and intellectual appeal of a religious quest'.[25] It would include such diverse thinkers as Thoreau, Walt Whitman, and Martin Luther King. The political spectrum of the Jeremiad would include left and right, conservatives and revolutionaries, with both accusing each other of having failed to realise the American dream. With such an interpretation, Bercovitch sees the rhetoric of the Jeremiad as an inclusive one – led by the idea that consensus leads to progress, with progress leading to betterment, with betterment leading towards the last fulfilment – salvation. Transferred into profane and secular language the American Jeremiad became 'a ritual of progress through consensus, a system of sacred–secular symbols . . . a "civil religion" for a people chosen to spring fully formed into the modern world – America . . . the only country that developed, from the seventeenth through the nineteenth centuries, into a wholly middle-class culture'.[26]

At the heart of Bercovitch's argument is the process of the transformation of geography into eschatology. As with Tocqueville, he rejects the human geography argument and like his predecessor he is concerned with the religious foundations and roots of American democracy; yet he differs in that he emphasises the role religious thought played in creating a consensus. Thus he is less concerned with the somewhat static view of religion; it is rather the notion of change while maintaining structure that occupies him. An old rhetoric had to be applied to new conditions – but only in order to control change. In this process the sacred and the profane became constantly entwined: 'The Yankee Jeremiahs took advantage of this movement "from sacred to profane" to shift the focus of figural authority. In effect they incorporated Bible history into the American experience – they substituted a regional for a biblical past, consecrated the American present as a movement from promise to fulfilment, and translated fulfilment from its meaning within the closed system of sacred history into a metaphor for limitless secular improvement'.[27] In such a system, radicalism became the affirmation of order. The ritual of consensus succeeded in incorporating the entire American political spectrum. Even the most radical voices of dissent tried to appeal to the rhetoric of the Jeremiad, the errand. It became a criticism without any alternative. Consequently the idea of the republic was not a contradiction or a threat to the American Jeremiad; in fact quite the opposite is true, it actually helped in building a consensus under which the young American republic could thrive.

Notes

1. Edward Conrad and Harold Spaeth (ed.): *The Constitution of the United States* (Bicentennial Edition, New York: Barnes & Noble Books 1987), p. 54.
2. In his *Democracy in America* (London: Fontana Press 1994).
3. It must be acknowledged, however, that revolutionaries like Thomas Paine and Thomas Jefferson were Deists. They did not believe in established, organised forms of religion, yet they certainly believed in some higher form of being that could be found in nature. Deism can be understood as a middle position between religion and complete atheistic forms of enlightenment. Such a middle position could certainly explain why the framers of the American Constitution drew a clear line between the framework of the American political system and the religious beliefs to be found in American civil society. Hence, the preamble of the Constitution does not start with 'God gave us . . .' but with 'We the people . . .'. Having said that, it must be pointed out that the Declaration of Independence mentions 'The Creator' – whoever that may be.
4. Tocqueville stresses that it was this constellation that proved so successful – not the specific geographical conditions and/or human geography.
5. *Democracy in America* p. 448.
6. *The Protestant Sects and The Spirit of Capitalism* was only published posthumously. I refer here to the text published in the Max Weber edition that has been edited by Hans Gerth and C. Wright Mills: *From Max Weber* (New York: Oxford University Press 1946).
7. Ibid. p. 312.
8. *Redeeming American Political Thought* (Chicago: Chicago University Press 1998).
9. Ibid. p. 129.
10. Ibid. p. 131f.
11. Ibid. p. 132.
12. Ibid. p. 133.

13. Ibid. p. 135.
14. Ibid. p. 137.
15. Ibid. p. 138.
16. *The New England Mind* (Cambridge, MA: The Belknap Press of Harvard University Press 1953); *Errand into the Wilderness* (Cambridge, MA: Harvard University Press 1956).
17. *The New England Mind* p. vii.
18. Both quotes in ibid. p. 14.
19. Ibid. p. 19.
20. Ibid. p. 29.
21. Ibid. p. 40.
22. *Errand into the Wilderness*, p. 9.
23. *The American Jeremiad* (Madison, WI: University of Wisconsin Press 1978), p. xii.
24. Ibid. this quote and the penultimate quote, p. 4f.
25. Ibid. p. 11.
26. Ibid. p. 28.
27. Ibid. p. 93f.

Chapter 3

Republicanism

The Federalists' interpretation of republicanism ● Pocock's link between Florentine political thought and the newly established American republic ● Arendt's republicanism: only the homo politicus can establish a realm of freedom ● Shklar's insistence on other influences: Montesquieu

It is a long way from the classic notion of Republicanism to the birth of the American republic. Consequently, from the Federalists to modern political theorists attempts have been made to identify both continuity and rupture in the reasoning on American republicanism. In what follows we will first look at attempts by the framers of the American Constitution to situate themselves in the republican tradition; we will then take a closer look at contemporary interpretations of American republicanism (in particular those of John G. A. Pocock, Hannah Arendt and Judith Shklar).

Apart from the Constitution itself, the most important document providing insight into the intellectual world of the Founding Fathers is the public defence of the constitutional agreement that was reached at the Philadelphia Convention. It was in *The Federalist Papers* that James Madison, Alexander Hamilton and John Jay discussed how the new constitutional arrangements fitted into historical republican traditions.[1]

Republican ideas were widely discussed owing to the fact that the English monarchy was the political form Americans were fighting against. But the focus was not only on alternatives that knew no crown and aristocracy but also on other options for conceiving of and establishing a political framework that would conform to the peculiar American circumstances. Thus, American conditions made it necessary to rethink and redefine republican ideas. It was in this context that the Founding Fathers – James Madison in particular – explored and discussed the rich political tradition of Europe, from the examples of Greece, Italy, Switzerland, and the Netherlands to political philosophers such as Montesquieu.

Madison (Publius) distinguished between a democracy where 'the people meet and exercise the government in person', and a republic where the people 'assemble and administer (the government) by their representatives and agents'.[2] The first case obviously referred to smaller places such as Athens, Switzerland and the North Italian city-states while the second form corresponded more to the unique American circumstances. For Madison, America gave a new meaning to the republican idea – and thereby also helped to redefine democracy under modern conditions. According to Publius, classic democracy thrived on the close physical relationship that existed between the citizens and the decision-making body (usually the assembly of citizens). A republic, he argued further, functions on the basis of representatives and is not necessarily bound to the size of city-states. As Madison stresses, America was unique in that it was so large in size and thus differed from Europe – and thus challenged the classic notion of the republic. At the same time Madison, Hamilton, Jay and most of the other framers of the Constitution wanted to retain the main principles of republicanism, namely that a republic should consist of a government that gained its power from society at large, and not just from one particular stratum, as in the European precedent.

In the attempt to overcome the contradiction, Madison, Hamilton and Jay referred to federalism and the separation of powers. The federal form guaranteed that representation would be fair in that it would take into account the geographical size of all the states (those that were part of the Union, plus those that would join in future) as well as the individual proportions of the present and future state populations; the task of the separation of powers was to balance and channel different class interests. Thus, Madison and the other Founding Fathers defined the American republic not only in opposition to what he conceived to be the classic European model of republicanism; they also contributed to the redefinition of democracy under new conditions.

Yet one should not judge the new republic only on the terms it invented for its own purposes. It is therefore necessary to take a more in-depth look and to discuss how contemporary intellectual historians have summarised America. The most enlightened source for analysing the republican strand in American thought and how it is linked to the older European traditions of republicanism is to be found in the work of John G. A. Pocock.

In his study of *The Machiavellian Moment – Florentine Political Thought and the Atlantic Republican Tradition* Pocock follows that same continuous republican line of reasoning that has its roots in the North Italian city-states, and which was then discussed in the British context (without success, in terms of establishing lasting political power) and, finally, via Britain made its way to the newly founded American republic.[3] Within this republican tradition, Pocock does not see radical ruptures but rather continuity, modification and revision. However, he concedes that, particularly in the American context, modification and revision were more likely to occur than unquestioned acceptance of and reliance on Europe's past. This led to a complex constellation that can be summarised as follows:

1. American thought must be understood in the context of British oppositional thought.

2. This thought itself had a history stretching back to the Aristotelian and Machiavellian tradition.

3. The breakaway from Britain and the newly found independence necessitated the reformulation or adaptation of the classic tradition.

As has been pointed out, Pocock's arguments differ from other arguments that interpret the American Revolution exclusively in terms of either absolute rupture or absolute continuity. This becomes especially clear in Pocock's treatment of the classic republican rhetoric of virtue applied to the American experience. Pocock discusses three aspects in particular: how to avoid corruption, the constitutional arrangements preventing corruption, and the Frontier, which can be considered as the American version of empire-building and which allowed virtue to thrive once the 'arrangements' were clear.

With respect to corruption versus virtue, the historical situation in which the Americans found themselves provided the background for a reformulation of the classic assumptions which could be described as almost ideal: being of mainly dissident English background, the arguments over taxation without representation only confirmed what the settlers had experienced before – namely that the British system was corrupt. In the new context of a colony seeking independence, corruption could now be externalised: it was the other side, the mother country that was corrupt. To avoid poisonous corruption, independence became the order of the day. It was only through independence that Americans could remain virtuous. Pocock reminds us that the Americans compared the situation of the British Empire to that of ancient Rome. Rome, which had once been a republic and had turned into a despotic regime where citizens became corrupt, not least through the assumption that the entire empire would work only for Rome. To be sure, there was nothing inherently wrong in building an empire; what *was* misguided however, was the supremist attitude that assumed that others would do the work. That was precisely what Americans would not expect from colonisation. Being familiar with their own form of discovery and empire-building in the West, Americans were well aware that in their context colonisation meant hard work. It was the assumption of a British hereditary monarchy profiteering from an empire where others did the work that disgusted the Americans in particular and consequently they would turn against the political form which seemed to be at the root of the problem. In contrast to the British system of parliamentary monarchy, the Americans experimented first with a confederation of republics; then, with the failure of the early confederation and compounded by the lack of a natural aristocracy that would have guaranteed such a confederation, they finally developed another idea. At the core of this idea was the concept of a unitary vision of 'the people' as sovereign. Yet 'the people' was an abstraction, particularly when seen in such monistic form; in reality, what was understood by 'the people', had become highly differentiated. To close the gap between normativity and reality, representation was 'invented'. As Pocock points out, with representation the Americans were already distancing themselves from classic thought and models and were in the middle of redefining and modernising republicanism.

However, republican virtue still remained a problem: the Founding Fathers thought themselves virtuous enough, since they themselves were that same natural aristocracy they dreamed about; the problem was the 'real people' who could not be fully trusted – and representation would not automatically ensure virtuous behaviour. Furthermore, increased commerce and related interests could potentially conflict with political action. The best insurance would thus consist of a plurality of modes within the political process – a system of checks and balances within the executive, legislative and judiciary branches of government. Such a plurality of modes would ensure that all interests were represented; it would also ensure that there was not one particular power or branch that could gain complete hegemony; and, finally, would ensure that a natural aristocracy could still emerge. In short: the institutional framework would be as complex as the civil society it represented; at the same time republican virtues, as now redefined in the context of interests, could still flourish. Pocock regards this 'liberal' redefinition of republicanism as more than just a simple paradigm change: no longer did the citizens participate directly in the affairs that had an impact on their lives, and neither the individual nor 'the people' was directly involved in governmental affairs. Yet the model also had obvious advantages: the new republic could absorb and channel the different passions of modern civil society much more effectively than the classic model could ever have done. With the new model the passions and the interests mingled, and virtue and fortune were no longer in contradiction. The institutional arrangements of the new republic guaranteed that change and stability were not mutually exclusive but actually became mutually beneficial. Even the western expansion of the Frontier did not pose a threat; the new republican empire could even expand to continental proportions – without repeating Rome's fall from virtuous grace.

According to Pocock, two further aspects helped to give birth to the revised American form of republicanism: the equality of condition (as discussed by Tocqueville) and a peculiar form of political theology, the American Jeremiad (as described by Bercovitch). Equality of subjection had been the classic form in republican thought on equality, yet this changed radically with the emergence of the American republic, as the emphasis on the equality of conditions was a challenge to republican thought. As Pocock points out: 'When men had been differentiated and had expressed their virtue in the act of deferring to one another's virtues, the individual had known himself through the respect shown by his fellows for the qualities publicly recognised in him; but once men were, or it was held that they ought to be, all alike, his only means of self-discovery lay in conforming to everybody else's opinion, since nothing but diffused general opinion now defined the ego or its standards of judgement'.[4] Pocock agrees here with Tocqueville's comments and concerns regarding the problem of the possibility of a tyranny of the majority, yet Pocock differs from Tocqueville's view of the tyranny of the majority developing from democratic ideas, because he interprets them in the context of republican ideas. The second aspect, that of political theology, is more difficult to conceptualise. While it is true that the development of the Frontier allowed virtue to blossom, the end of internal colonisation could also pose a threat to republican thought. As Pocock stresses: 'Even in America, the republic faces the problem of its own ultimate finitude, and that of its virtue, in space and time.'[5] The only safeguard against such endings would lie in an infinite future, a future that would bind together the past and the present in both a messianistic and cyclical way. Particularly in times of crisis, the rhetoric of Jeremiad would help to revitalise the republican spirit. Yet, as Pocock stresses, such an option would be in conflict with another more realistic-practical republican strand of reasoning (promoted by Founding Fathers such as Madison); in extreme circumstances such reasoning could even turn against the Constitution itself. To understand such internal contradictions within American republicanism, Pocock suggests interpreting the specific Jeremiadian rhetoric in context. American society was only on the brink of becoming modern society, and, as he himself tried to show, it tried to come to terms with the new conditions by relying on political concepts that stemmed from a Machiavellian, European past. Relying on this tradition, the force of other competing social thought – be it Hegelian or Marxist or both – would never play a central role in the American republic.

As can be seen, American 'ideology' did not change, even though America changed from an agriculturally and trade-dominated society to a modern industrial society. Following Hannah Arendt, Pocock regards

America as a country that defined and still continues to define itself in purely classic political terms; the homo politicus was its major concern, not the homo faber – hence no Hegel, no Marx and no final struggle.

As has been stated in the context of exceptionalism, Hannah Arendt interpreted the American experience as one that emphasised 'the political' against 'the social'. For Arendt, the establishment of the American republic and the Constitution served as a permanent institutional insurance and reminder that 'the political' and the realm of freedom had prevailed and would always be successful against 'the social' and the realm of necessities (as had been the case in the French Revolution). According to Arendt, the success of the establishment of the American republic can only be understood when one looks at the different legitimisation patterns: in France, theoretically and practically, the republic thought of acting in accordance with the people's *volonté general*; in America the people were perceived theoretically as one but practically as a multitude with various interests.[6] Hannah Arendt proves her point by stressing that although the American Founding Fathers conceived of 'the people' as being sovereign constitutionally they never appealed direct to the general public opinion for action, as the French revolutionaries did. There simply was no need to appeal to the entire general public, because the majority of Americans were not haunted by privileged positions resulting from class wars and the poverty that the majority of the French, the third estate, had suffered from. In a way, the American Revolution was blessed in that the conceptualisation of the republic ostensibly took place in an ivory tower, with the Founding Fathers unconcerned with questions of social necessities. The meeting at Philadelphia could take place in an almost seminar-like atmosphere – certainly not free of political demands, but certainly free of the social pressures that the French revolutionaries were under. In such an atmosphere political virtues could flourish mainly because they did not translate directly into social virtues, as they did in the French instance. In France, the *volonté general* demanded virtues in every individual – a prerequisite that stemmed from the language of necessities; consequently, a general suspicion developed and terror was the solution. In contrast, no *terreur* ever developed in America. According to Arendt the differences in conceptions of what constitutes the *res publica* can also be attributed to different pre-revolutionary experiences. Whereas in France the people knew of republican ideas through the enlightened writings of their *hommes de lettres*, but had no practical experiences in conducting their own affairs, in America people had gained practical experience in their townhall meetings. These townhall meetings were not abolished in the institutional design of the new republic. In contrast, as a part of the federal structure, they became an integral part of the

American political process – thereby guaranteeing the experience of spontaneity and other positive effects of direct involvement in public affairs.

The different historical experiences also said a lot about the differing interpretations of republicanism of the respective intellectual traditions of the two countries. While intellectuals in France were detached from the common people and indeed from practical politics, American intellectuals were directly involved in public affairs. In other words, while the intellectuals in France perpetuated a class system within the newly established French republic, this was not the case in America. Arendt does not deny the distinguished role and social position of the American Founding Fathers, yet she insists that they were 'organic' republican intellectuals and hence did not form a distinct class. Arendt insists that in the last instance, the American intellectuals and Founding Fathers could conceptualise and institutionally guarantee political freedom because they themselves obeyed nobody and were free; only as equals and citizens were they in a position to promise themselves and each other the pursuit of public happiness. It is this idea of political equality that, according to Arendt, was so unique to the idea on the American republic. It is the emphasis of the equation of homo politicus = political equality = citizenship = public happiness and public life (as opposed to homo faber = social equality = subjectship = private happiness and private life) that highlights the different conceptions of republicanism in America compared to France. To be sure, there were reasons why Arendt focused so much on 'the political'; but to consider the new American republic solely in political terms necessarily led to the neglect of other aspects – aspects that would later be discussed in liberal thought. Thus, before turning to liberalism as an American political tradition, it is useful to refer to a thinker who is known for her commitment to liberal ideas and traditions but who also acknowledged the role of republican ideas in the formation of the United States' political framework.

In her posthumously published collections of essays, Judith Shklar takes issue with the intellectual influences of the Founding Fathers.[7] In particular, she reminds us that the framers of the American Constitution were exposed to a wide range of classical thought, reaching from Aristotelian logic to knowledge about classical republican forms of government. Additionally, Americans knew that if a republic was to be successful, it would be one that would not simply refer to and repeat the mistakes of the republics that had existed in Europe; Americans were quite aware of the advantages and historical progress that had been made by countries such as Britain with its mixed forms of government consisting of a monarch, lords and commons. Thus, Americans had a sense of progress in history and they clearly saw their republic as contributing to even further progress. Shklar here takes a unique middle position between Pocock and Arendt. While Pocock emphasises the new but, in the last instance, cyclical form of American republicanism (mainly derived from the reliance by a new formation in unique historical circumstances on pre-modern Machiavellian republican traditions), Arendt differs in that she emphasises again and again the absolute beginning, the fresh start. The carefully balanced position of Shklar combines both views: 'It is . . . meant not to deny that the Founders reflected frequently and deeply upon the political history of European antiquity, but to note that it was by considering that remote past that they came to realise fully how very novel their project was, and to give the phrase *Novus ordo seculorum* its full impact.'[8]

But what exactly allowed the Founding Fathers to combine and critically apply classic republican thought to the new, quite unique conditions and circumstances they found in America? According to Shklar, it is the intellectual influence of Montesquieu that proved to be decisive in this respect. The argument put forward in the French philosopher's book *The Spirit of the Laws* was the political currency of the day – an influence that was by no means limited to Europe but which was also appreciated in America. From Britain's experience Montesquieu borrowed and elaborated the idea of the rule of law and the idea of mixed government – ideas that could not be further from classic republican thought. The rule of law drew a line between public and private life, meaning that for the first time ever only certain actions would be subject to the rule of law, while other actions would be left to society's self-regulating bodies; the mixed form of government suggested a carefully drawn constitutional arrangement with a separation of powers, particularly an independent judiciary. Another new element was that the British government had made systematic attempts to cope with the demands of commerce – another important feature that did not play a major role in classic republican thought. While Shklar concedes that Montesquieu's interpretation of Britain was very often overstated and sometimes even based on misunderstandings, she also points out that it is Montesquieu who must be credited for having discussed these points in a systematic way. The Federalists, according to Shklar, took all this for granted and elaborated upon the ideas of the French philosopher in order to make them applicable to American circumstances. The classic examples of republicanism were used as a reference point to highlight mistakes that the American republic should avoid. Thus, the idea of a confederation of republics was rejected in favour of a union in which the problem of size would be dealt with through proper representation; in terms of civic republican attitudes, the idea of virtue was replaced by the idea of consent 'with diverse interests and a shared concern for life, liberty, and the security of property'.[9] To be sure, Shklar departed radically here from the republican line of reasoning found in Pocock and Arendt. The paradigm change from Machiavelli to Montesquieu is an indication of this change. Shklar's reference to Montesquieu and the interpretation of his work through the Founding Fathers clarified that republicanism would have to incorporate liberal ideas or else it would not have a future – at least not on the American continent. But what this liberal republicanism also demonstrated was the emergence of modern society and the problems that come with the organisation of social life within it. The point to be made is that the rise of 'the social' was something that did not stop at the borders of the newly founded American republic.

Notes

1. *The Federalist Papers* first appeared in 1788. I refer here to the edition published in London and New York: Penguin 1987.
2. Ibid. p. 141.
3. *The Machiavellian Moment* (Princeton, NJ: Princeton University Press 1975).
4. Ibid. p. 537f.
5. Ibid. p. 541f.
6. *On Revolution* (New York: Viking Press 1963).
7. *Redeeming American Political Thought* (Chicago: Chicago University Press 1998); *Political Thought and Political Thinkers* (Chicago: Chicago University Press 1998).
8. Ibid. p. 158.
9. Ibid. p. 165.

Chapter 4

Liberalism

Comprehensive approaches to liberalism: Louis Hartz and James P. Young • Hartz's conceptualisation of exceptionalist liberalism • Bringing republicanism and other influences back in: Young's revision of Hartz • Minimalist approaches: John Rawls and Judith Shklar • Rawls' political liberalism in the context of his general political philosophy: more pluralism • Shklar's conception of late liberalism: the 'liberalism of fear' • Enabling citizens through constraints: Stephen Holmes' 'finishing touch' of Shklar • The rejection of the alternative 'Rechtsstaat' versus 'Sozialstaat'

There are two main approaches to comprehending American liberalism. The first is a 'comprehensive' approach which suggests that liberalism might be an all-embracing American ideology that, having become differentiated over the course of the nineteenth and twentieth centuries, explains all facets of America's social and political life. The main representatives of such a view are the political scientists Louis Hartz and James P. Young. The second is a more philosophically grounded 'minimalist' approach, which is opposed to the comprehensive view in that it attempts to be analytically more sophisticated and thus sharper in its political and social distinctions. The political philosophers John Rawls and Judith Shklar represent this second view.

Discussing liberalism in America, Louis Hartz occupies the same prominent place that Alexis de Tocqueville and Seymour Martin Lipset occupy in the context of American exceptionalism and John G. A. Pocock in the context of republicanism. Thus, every account of the history and relevance of American liberal thought has to begin with Hartz's groundbreaking study *The Liberal Tradition in America*.[1]

Hartz openly acknowledges the Tocquevillean influence in his work, and agrees with his predecessor that America's distinguishing feature is indeed its lack of feudal institutions – with the result that America never had to fight against an oppressive regime. Since there was no need for a revolutionary approach, liberal ideas had the opportunity to flourish. For the same reasons,

America also knows no genuine conservative tradition, ' "born equal" . . . (America) lacks . . . a tradition of reaction.'[2] Yet, as Hartz argues further, there are two sides to the coin, 'for a society which begins with Locke, and thus transforms him, stays with Locke, by virtue of an absolute and irrational attachment it develops for him.'[3] Thus, while in Europe the origins of socialism and the demand for radical social equality go back to feudalist times and the fight against an *ancien régime*, no such tradition could develop in America. For Hartz, the absence of any real alternative, be it conservative or socialist, functions as a double-edged sword; precisely because liberalism had become second nature to Americans, a substantial void developed within American thought. This emptiness would have its particular implications when situations arose which called for America to see itself critically, as this void meant that there was no other perspective and no sense of relativity. It is in this respect that America still needed Europe in that they could together provide mutual enlightenment, if only to increase awareness of their own realities. As Hartz notes: 'America represents the liberal mechanism of Europe functioning without the European social antagonisms, but the truth is, it is only through these antagonisms that we recognise the mechanism.'[4] Hartz's study goes on to elaborate upon this distinction.

As has already been said, the remarkable feature of the American Revolution was less that it had led to freedom, but more that it did not have to deal with feudal structures; it thus experienced the luxury of a 'soft' revolution that had had no need to be excessive in its means in order to be successful, nor did it have to set an example for the world. It is in this respect that the further development of American social and political thought transgressed from the European example. In contrast to French and Russian revolutionaries and thinkers, one encounters an almost 'pragmatic' attitude in the reasoning of the Founding Fathers. To Hartz, this comes as no surprise. Until the events that led to the War of Independence, the Americans simply had no use for radical rhetoric. Social and political thought was rather traditional and Puritan. Political radicals like Thomas Paine proved to be the exception. The same holds true for early entrepreneurial middle-class thinkers: 'Benjamin Franklins in fact, the Americans did not have to become Jeremy Benthams in theory.'[5] Hartz explains the absence of any radical rhetoric with the early social and political success of the American middle class. In fact, Hartz goes so far as to state that the American middle class was so triumphant in 1776 that it took its secure future for granted.[6]

Being essentially middle class in her aspirations and expectations, America is usually regarded as a society with an individualistic culture. In general,

Hartz agrees with such a view but also sides with Tocqueville in pointing out that there are also strong uniformistic tendencies. If liberalism was the standard, any deviation and dissent from the standard notion of what it means to be free could have detrimental consequences. Tocqueville called this 'the tyranny of the majority'. Hartz elaborates on this observation, noting that the concept of freedom contains both variety and equality. In his view, it was only through a peculiar twist of history that the two became separated – with Europe opting for variety (Hartz calls this the Burkean option) and America opting for equality (which Hartz calls the Paine option). With this 'division of labour' between the two continents, conservatism was never given a chance to develop in America: 'While millions of Europeans have fled to America to discover the freedom of Paine, there have been few Americans . . . who have fled to Europe to discover the freedom of Burke.'[7]

But the spectrum of the American approach to liberalism can best be described by looking at the example of the interpretation of the writings of John Locke – the liberal thinker par excellence. Locke's political philosophy originally developed within a European framework. Its aim was to introduce the idea of limited government against the arbitrariness of the concept of absolutism. Transferred to America, the part of Locke that dealt with normative arguments suddenly changed into a description of a reality: 'The social norms of Europe (became) the factual premises of America'.[8] While in Europe the idea of social liberty became the crucial driving force behind the revolutions, in America it served merely as a starting point. On the basis of this historical difference, the idea of the 'reality of atomistic social freedom' developed.[9] According to Hartz, this concept of atomistic social freedom finds its presupposition in political liberty and equality actually existing. Again the comparison with Europe highlights America's distinctiveness: it is only through the reflection of the different preconditions – social inequality in Europe and political equality in America – that one is able to analyse the peculiar social dimensions of the American Revolution.[10]

Hartz demonstrates the American distinctiveness by referring to two typical American revolutionaries, the farmer and the artisan. According to Hartz, both examples show that political equality had an impact on the way social freedom was perceived: 'We see in the very nature of the social forces which went into the personality of the American radical the non-feudal world from which he derives his strength. This "petit-bourgeois" was centrally a man of the land, a small capitalist in the American backwoods, breathing the Jacobin spirit of the "shop" as it were, in a novel agrarian setting. Nothing in the French peasantry, and certainly in the English tenant, could compare with the way the American farmer absorbed the land into small-scale capitalism . . . The artisan, too, in the East, showed a liberal, non-proletarian orientation pregnant with significance for the New World.'[11] What Hartz demonstrates here is that the only enemy the farmer and the artisan had were the richer liberals – not a king or an aristocracy as in France or Russia. What his example further demonstrates is that all conflicts in America must be interpreted as conflicts within the hegemonic paradigm of liberalism. Once the major underlying arguments have been presented and distinctions have been made, Hartz just has to apply his conceptual tools to the historical process. Thus, in the course of the early American republic the struggle was not between an upper class consisting of an aristocracy or a bourgeoisie and a lower class consisting of a peasantry or a proletariat; rather, the struggle took place between a liberal upper middle class and a demo-cratic lower middle class. Such a constellation made the invention of a category such as 'petit-bourgeoisie' absurd. As has been stressed before, in America the situation was different; in the words of Hartz, here it was 'the peasant . . . transformed into a capitalist farmer, and the labourer . . . transformed into an incipient entrepreneur' that created a 'great new democratic hybrid unknown in any other land'.[12] All further conflicts, first between Republicans and Federalists, then between the Democratic–Republican Party (later known as the Democratic Party) and Whigs, and finally between Democrats and Republicans, can thus be interpreted as social struggles within the liberal consensus as defined by Hartz.

The struggle over agrarian capitalism versus the urban–industrial form in the late eighteenth century and in the early nineteenth century, and later in the twentieth century between laissez-faire capitalism and state intervention in the economy, must be seen as arguments between a reform-minded liberalism and a 'whiggish' form of liberalism. Even the extreme case of slavery in the South fits into this picture of hegemonic liberalism: slavery in the South always remained slavery, that is it could never penetrate the liberals' mind; its practical weakness and its defeat were directly linked to its weak theoretical stand; directly opposed to liberal ideas, it could never develop into a viable alternative, into a social system that would not be based on the assumption of natural inequality, inhuman submission and enslavement of a large part of its population. In other words, the South could not survive, as it had no liberal foundation.

Louis Hartz's account of liberalism as the sole American political tradition did not remain unchallenged. In his study *Reconsidering American Liberalism* James P. Young attempted a radical revision of the liberalism thesis.[13] He accused Hartz of having painted a too homogeneous and monolithic picture. In particular, the critic hinted at four points which were either neglected or not properly addressed. First, Hartz's account begins with the

American Revolution and thus neglects Puritanism as one of the most important influences. Young concedes that the Puritans could hardly be called 'liberals'; yet he maintains that the Puritans' action had unintended consequences and finally helped liberalism to emerge. The rule of law, modern individualism and voluntarism would be unthinkable without the Puritans' commitment to community life and conducting their own affairs. Second, Hartz neglects the considerable hierarchies that existed in pre-revolutionary America. In particular, Young criticises Hartz's superficial treatment of the South. As a matter of fact, one can hardly talk seriously of American liberalism while segregation still existed. Third, Hartz seems to completely neglect the issue of republicanism. As in the case of Puritanism, Young stresses that republicanism is usually not considered to be part of the liberal agenda; he points out that any account of American liberalism will have to assimilate the attention that the American Founding Fathers paid to the classic republican tradition. Having said that, Young is aware of Pocock's and other scholars' arguments that see Lockean liberal theory as having been surpassed by the Founding Fathers' re-interpretation of Machiavellian civic humanism – a neo-classic line of thinking which had come to America through James Harrington and the English republicans. Young agrees in part with this argument in that he states that, while it is true that the Founding Fathers' reasoning focused on the past experiences of the European republics and that the Founding Fathers sympathised with the republican virtue of participation in political affairs, they were at the same time aware of the problems posed by the shortcomings of the classic European models, which were unable to accommodate the implications of a vast geography and the element of increased commerce therein. In summary, Young sees the benefits and influences of American republican-ism, but disagrees with Pocock's radical conclusion. In his own account, Young sees republicanism mediated through the Puritan ethic and the Lockean ideas with their emphasis on natural rights. Young reminds us in particular of the criticism of the anti-federalists who voiced republican views that resembled those of Rousseau. Fourth, Young also stresses the con-flictual dimensions in American politics and society against Hartz's portrait of liberal consensus. Both consensus and conflict are integral part of American politics. Thus, while it is true that the Lockean social contract is a contract based on a consensus among political equals, it is also true that the realisation of this contract did not lead to a conflict-free society. As a matter of fact, America always knew conflict – from the American Revolution to the Civil War, from the debate on modern civil rights to twentieth-century industrial disputes.

To summarise then, Young's accusation is that Hartz's interpretation of liberalism is not sufficiently differentiated; it does not distinguish between liberalism and democracy, nor does it take the many liberalisms in American history into account, that is the classic liberal idea as first promoted by John Locke, economic liberalism and political economy from the founder Adam Smith to contemporary advocates such as Milton Friedman and, finally, reform-minded liberalism from John Stuart Mill to John Dewey and John Rawls. It is complexity that Young finds lacking in Hartz. Yet to insist on complexity in itself does not provide an explanation. As a matter of fact, Young's own historically minded account of liberalism is in grave danger of embracing every modern aspect of American society whilst explaining none. As the second part of this chapter tries to demonstrate, this weakness in Young's and Hartz's argument is only overcome by more rigid thinking, as demonstrated by such distinguished political philosophers as John Rawls and Judith Shklar.

The two studies that turned Harvard professor John Rawls into America's most distinguished philosopher are *A Theory of Justice* and *Political Liberalism*. Both studies led to the revival of a branch of philosophy that until the appearance of Rawls' groundbreaking contributions had been pronounced dead – political philosophy. Rawls' attempts can best be described as attempts to rethink the very political foundations under which we live today. Such philosophical efforts are necessarily abstract; they must have a full understanding of modern society yet reduce its complexity. Thus, *Political Liberalism* does not aim at a comprehensive understanding of the structure of liberalism actually existing in the United States (as do Hartz' and Young's studies); rather, it discusses the minimal requirements and preconditions that make us support the framework called 'political liberalism'.[14]

When questioning how Rawls perceives political liberalism and why it holds such importance from him, one has to look at Rawls' first study, *A Theory of Justice*, where the assumption of a well-ordered society was central to the overall argument. In *Political Liberalism* Rawls states that he now no longer believes in this argument – as he recognises that we now live in a pluralist social world and society with competing, often irreconcilable views. Yet as Rawls points out, we still live this social life under a political umbrella – a framework that is based on an overlapping political consensus. It is this larger framework which he seeks to understand and explain.[15]

Reflecting on the preconditions necessary to achieve political liberalism, Rawls presents the reader with his methodological approach, the idea of the 'original position'. The original position takes on the form of an almost Weberian-like ideal type: it serves to clarify ideas and positions and thus helps us 'to work out what we think'; the original position also forces us to systematise our ideas, to relate different ideas and levels of ideas to one another and thus brings 'greater coherence among all our judgements'.[16] After having introduced the form of his argument, Rawls returns to discussing content and opens by discussing a number of fundamental ideas that are prerequisites and preconditions for the development of political liberalism. He draws a distinction between the notion of being reasonable versus being rational. Rawls argues that we are reasonable in our individual expectations, which encourages reciprocity and in turn leads to the idea of fair co-operation. In contrast, being rational, that is, relying on solipsistic forms of thinking, mostly in terms of instrumental means–ends relationships, does not lead to the same reciprocal and social expectations. Rawls' insistence on reasonableness leads to another idea – that of the public and public reasoning.[17] Reasonable reciprocal relationships depend on the burden of judgement. This notion implies that these relationships must be public; reasonableness may only be judged and justified by others. Yet to be reasonable requires another important precondition; one can only reason in public among equals. This in turn implies political equality, that is citizenship and some form of constitutional 'guidelines', or rules and regulations. Once in place, it is these institutionalised forms which guarantee political autonomy. As a result, a 'self-regulating' political system is established, which in turn nourishes its constitutive parts.

In the second part of his book, Rawls elaborates a theme which he touched on earlier – the idea of an overlapping consensus. According to Rawls, the overlapping consensus must be explicitly political, as the social realm, that is civil society, is too divided and too diverse to provide a consensus. As Rawls stresses: 'The political is distinct from the associational, which is voluntary in ways that the political is not; it is also distinct from the personal and the familial, which are affectional, again in ways the political is not.'[18] To remain stable, the political consensus must be laid down within a constitutional framework.

Linked integrally to the idea of the consensus and its related constitutional framework is the idea of rights. In the words of Rawls, the idea of rights consists of 'the same rights, liberties and opportunities, and the same all-purpose means such as income and wealth, with all of these supported by the same social bases of self-respect.'[19] It is the idea of rights which guarantees the functioning of the framework – not just in terms of formal equality but in terms of minimal substantial equality. Having said that, one has to bear in mind that Rawls discusses only the preconditions for participation in a liberal framework, he does not discuss good life as a whole. However, Rawls recognised the necessity of a minimum social agenda which would be politically guaranteed; if this were not the case, no unity in terms of basic liberal political consensus could be held up against the diversity and heterogeneity of civil society.

The other idea that Rawls comes back to and elaborates upon is the idea of public reasoning. Yet in contrast to his earlier discussion of public reasoning as a precondition of political liberalism, he now addresses public reasoning from an institutional viewpoint. As Rawls explains, 'the political' rests not on private but on shared public concerns – hence his emphasis on fundamental political equality guaranteed through citizenship. Yet public reasoning is not solely guaranteed by voluntary participation and public-minded citizens. In a constitutional democracy conflictual situations can arise where public reasoning takes on the form of institutionalised public reasoning; it does so by judicial interpretations. Rawls reminds us that the courts could not act if they were not legitimised and if they were not based on an overall consensus that sometimes forces citizens to obey the rules of the political 'game'. It is in this respect that we become aware that we have gone full circle. As Rawls points out: 'higher law is the expression of the people's constituent power and has the higher authority of the will of We the People.'[20] The central idea here is that political liberalism clearly rejects the idea of the legislative supremacy of an 'absolutist' parliament and it becomes clear that it is the American not the British model that serves as a guideline for his conceptualisation of political liberalism.

In the final part of his work Rawls provides us with a synthesis of his views. He assures the reader that his argument had indeed gone full circle – not only within his conceptualisation of political liberalism but also in bringing his conception of justice in line with a political framework.[21] In his final remarks he refers back to his earlier arguments in his first study and maintains that his new conception of 'justice as fairness' is much more inclusive. It cannot be reduced simply to judicial concerns and questions of rights, but becomes part of a larger project – that of deliberative liberal democracy.

In contrast to John Rawls, who aims at reviving political liberalism through reviving the classic political philosophy tradition of John Locke and Immanuel Kant, the argument of Judith Shklar, who had been a Harvard colleague of Rawls, takes a different route. Her conceptualisation of liberalism is still a 'minimalist' one, yet it differs from Rawls in that it is an 'ex negativo' one that is very specific. Based on the American perception and interpretation of the European past, her 'liberalism of fear' refers more openly to distinct American experiences than Rawls' political liberalism.[22]

Shklar insists that historically liberalism is a latecomer. In Europe it is not older than the nineteenth century; in France it never became a powerful hegemonic force, and in Britain, where it was 'invented', it was never extended to the rest of the British Empire. In the case of the United States, it hardly makes sense to talk about liberalism as a political force before the end of the Civil War; and even afterwards, as Shklar points out, other political ideas dominated American public discourse.

Having noted the late arrival of liberalism as a reality, Skhlar is aware that liberal ideas are of course much older, stemming from a fear of cruelty in Europe's religious and civil wars. Tolerance and early liberal ideas grew out of the sheer necessity of avoiding the evil of these medieval wars. Later, the Enlightenment and the progress in the sciences helped to develop a helpful scepticism – which in turn helped to fight religious dogmatism and intolerance. Surprisingly, the political philosophers who are usually credited with the conceptualisation of liberalism – Locke and John Stuart Mill – do not play a role in Shklar's 'liberalism of fear'. The main reason that Shklar gives for this omission is that Locke and Mill do not belong to the 'party of memory' – a central concept in Shklar's reasoning. It is indeed historical memory, which is the motive and driving force behind the 'liberalism of fear'. It is the wish not to repeat the atrocities of the past. Locke and Mill had little to say in this respect.

Since an 'ex negativo' momentum is crucial for the understanding of the liberalism of fear, its political realisation does not require much; Shklar stresses the constitutionally granted separation of public and private life, political pluralism which guarantees access to political institutions and the elimination of extreme forms and degrees of social inequality as minimum requirements. Shklar's account of the liberalism of fear does not need a *summum bonum*; to function it needs only to remind citizens of the constant possibility of a *summum malum*. This, however, can only be a starting point, a first principle; but it is exactly this first principle which turns the 'liberalism of fear' into a universal enterprise, simply by assuming that everybody has an interest in avoiding 'arbitrary, unexpected, unnecessary and unlicensed acts of force and habitual and perversive acts of cruelty and torture.'[23] Such a principle is important not only because it can become part of a developing political morality; it is also important because there can be no debate about its underlying reasoning. It is a first principle because there can be no alternative to its acceptance and acknowledgement; liberalism's tolerance would have reached its end should someone attempt to violate it.

A direct result, or rather the intellectual sister of the first principle of avoiding cruelty, is the idea of rights. Shklar reminds us that the idea of rights is much more important to the history of American liberalism than the European liberal distinction between positive and negative liberty. This is so because the majority of the influential framers of the American constitution, particularly the Federalists, belonged to the party of memory; according to Shklar, they knew that in order to avoid the cruelty of the European past they had to interpret the American constitutional framework in a different fashion. They did not rely on their hope that government would not be arbitrary. Instead, they constructed a Bill of Rights, which explicitly states what government was not allowed to do. Eventually this Bill of Rights became the basis for demanding even more rights, thus taking a very different path from the English concept of negative liberty.

As is obvious, Shklar's conception of the liberalism of fear has different roots from Rawls' philosophical original position; yet, surprisingly, both 'minimalist' conceptualisations of liberalism come to the same conclusion in stressing rights, political equality, fairness, the distinction between private and public, and constitutionalism. Compared to the comprehensive view of liberalism as discussed by Hartz and Young, it also distinguishes between 'the political' and 'the social' (with a preference for the former), where no such clear distinction can be found in either Hartz or Young. It is rather the mingling of 'the social' with 'the political' that is the characteristic feature of the comprehensive view. The price they pay for this is high – they might well be in a position to spell out the distinctiveness of the American social and political system, but they are by no means in a position to abstract and universalise the ideas of American political liberalism.

It is Stephen Holmes, a political scientist from Princeton University and close associate of Judith Shklar, who deserves the credit for having responded appropriately to the questions and the criticism raised by Shklar and partly by Rawls. In many ways, Holmes' commentary on the theory of liberal democracy in his *Passions and Constraints* can be read as an attempt to synthesise both minimalist and comprehensive views.[24] Central to Holmes' argument is the Founding Fathers' early awareness of the benefits of constraints in the Constitution (particularly to be found in Hamilton and Madison's argument). This early introduction of constitutional constraints then led to the further discussion of the relationship between positive and negative liberty and – with the decision favouring the idea of positive liberty – to the modern idea of constitutionalism with its emphasis on rights. According to Holmes, the absence of state legislation does not necessarily enable citizens to enjoy their liberty (as hypothesised in most of the British tradition of negative liberty), rather it is the introduction of some principles (mostly in the form of 'gag' rules) that serve not only as a protection but that furthermore, have enabling functions. Whereas in the British model of 'the sovereignty of the parliament' most of the deliberation and certainly all the decision-making power is limited to the actual members of parliament (worse, in most cases it is actually only the majority which deliberates and decides), the American model allows deliberation to take place in a much broader fashion – not least, because the idea of 'the sovereignty of the people' and its practical insurance through federalist procedures and the separation of powers allow a much broader involvement of citizens in the deliberation process. As Holmes rightly stresses: 'It is meaningless to speak about popular government apart from some sort of legal framework which enables the electorate to express a coherent will. For this reason, democratic citizens require some organisational support from regime-founding forefathers. Unless they tie their own hands, with the help of their predecessors, 'the people' will be unable to deliberate effectively and act consistently.'[25] Again, Holmes refers here not only to Shklar's idea of the 'liberalism of fear' that aims foremost at the avoidance of cruelty; he also sees the idea of constitutional restraints as a positive force in that all further developments in terms of possible entitlements are derivations of it. As a result, modern constitutionalism redefined citizenship; it is no longer only the right to hold a passport, but is enabling in that it forms the very political ladder from which to climb into the realm of other (mostly social) rights. Once the main principles are established, the citizens are of course free – within 'certain predetermined channels' (Holmes) – to extend or limit further legislation, pending the interpretation of changing conditions. Within the possible alternatives that may arise, people should of course be free to disagree. The point is – and here Holmes echoes Rawls – that 'we can agree upon the right while differing on the good. To establish a public conception of justice, acceptable to all members of a diverse society, we must abstain from questions which elicit radical disagreement. In a liberal social order, "certain matters are reasonably taken off the political agenda".'[26] The insistence on the enabling potentialities of limited, constitutionally binding constraints also leads Holmes to redefine the relationship between a *Rechtsstaat* based on constitutional rights and a *Sozialstaat*, based on social or welfare rights. In his view, we tend to construe the two as opposed to each other, whereas we should rather rethink the relationship – not in terms of two conflicting rights, but rather as one where retributive rights become a precondition for all the other (mostly distributive) entitlements, such as government support. With this last comment Holmes has not only provided a sound explanation for the insistence of Americans to use the 'rhetoric of rights'; he also reminds us that this insistence has its firm roots in the American interpretation of liberal ideas.

Notes

1. *The Liberal Tradition in America* was first published in 1953. I refer here to an edition of the same text published in New York: Harcourt Brace Jovanovitch 1955.
2. Ibid. p. 5.

3. Ibid. p. 6.
4. Ibid. p. 16.
5. Ibid. p. 55.
6. Hartz immediately qualifies this argument: the very fact that the middle class was successful does not mean that America at the time did not have a stratified society; it only means that the 'aristocratic' stratum was not strong enough to cause the common people's anger that the French or Russian aristocracy had caused: 'Thus it happened that fundamental aspects of Europe's code of political thought met an ironic fate in the most bourgeois country in the world. They were not so much rejected as they were ignored' (p. 53).
7. *The Liberal Tradition in America*, p. 57.
8. Ibid. p. 60.
9. Ibid. p. 62.
10. In any other case one could make the mistake of explaining America's social conflicts by using tools inherited from Europe's social distinctions.
11. *The Liberal Tradition in America*, p. 74.
12. Ibid. p. 92.
13. *Reconsidering American Liberalism* (Boulder, CO: Westview Press 1996).
14. *Political Liberalism* (Cambridge, MA: Harvard University Press 1993), *A Theory of Justice* (Cambridge, MA: Harvard University Press 1971).
15. The very fact that we can agree on a framework called 'political liberalism' has been made possible by three interconnected developments: first, the Reformation, which led to religious pluralism, which then in turn became the precondition for modern forms of pluralism with its tolerance of differences and the freedom of thought and conscience; second, the rise of the modern nation state with its centralisation of power, which in turn triggered the rise of modern democratic and political institutions, including modern citizenship; third, the Enlightenment, which made us reasonable persons, largely influenced by the development of modern science.
16. Both quotes are from *Political Liberalism*, p. 26. Yet, although Rawls uses the universal philosophical language, there always remains the suspicion that he draws heavily on American experiences, or that he sees America as the model for the rest of the (Western) world.
17. To be reasonable one needs a reciprocal relationship consisting of at least one other person; the same is not true for rationality, where individuals can make up their own individual minds as to what constitutes rational action.
18. *Political Liberalism*, p. 137.
19. Ibid. p. 180.
20. Ibid. p. 231.
21. 'The original position connects the conception of the person and its companion conception of social co-operation with certain specific principles of justice.' (p. 304).
22. *Political Thought and Political Thinkers* (Chicago/London: University of Chicago

Press 1998); *Redeeming American Political Thought* (Chicago/London: University of Chicago Press 1998).

23. *Political Thought and Political Thinkers*, p. 11.
24. *Passions and Constraints* (Chicago/London: The University of Chicago Press 1995).
25. Ibid. p. 167.
26. Ibid. p. 203.

Chapter 5

Pragmatism

The forerunner of Pragmatism: Ralph Waldo Emerson ● Pragmatism and the development of higher education ● Peirce and the development of a Pragmatist method ● James: the populariser of Pragmatism ● The high peak of Pragmatism: John Dewey's 'The Public and its Problems' ● Liberalism, Pragmatism, and the reconstruction of the public sphere ● The discovery of 'the social' and further applications within the Pragmatist tradition: Thorstein Veblen and C. Wright Mills

In the preceding chapters the subject has been the modes and traditions in American social and political thought – exceptionalism, political theology as symbolised by the Jeremiad, republicanism and liberalism. For obvious reasons the discussion has been one of content rather than form. Yet, if the maxim is true that form is also condensed content, the legitimate question arises whether or not there is a genuine American way of thinking. Indeed, there is one particular strand of American social and political thought that fits this description – Pragmatism. In that which follows I will look only at the first of what has been called the 'two pragmatisms'.[1] The first Pragmatism has early roots that go back to the philosopher Ralph Waldo Emerson. Emerson laid the foundations, yet the problem was that Emerson's reflections were not delivered in a scientific or social scientific language. His thoughts were still very much formulated in a language that wasn't fully secularised. Only later, with the establishment of a more 'worldly' higher education system, could Pragmatism flourish. Charles Sanders Peirce became the pioneer; his thoughts on the pragmatic method were popularised by William James and reached its first peak with John Dewey and the discovery of 'the social'. The further application of pragmatist ideas to the social world at large was a project that was then later pursued by Thorstein Veblen and C. Wright Mills.

In his lectures and public addresses Ralph Waldo Emerson laid the foundations upon which Pragmatism would later thrive.[2] In his speeches one can already encounter the entire vocabulary of later Pragmatism. In one of his best known speeches, 'The American Scholar', he talks about the rejection of 'the courtly muses of Europe', the insistence on individualism and individual perception, and the consequences that the division of labour could have on the constitution of the 'intellect'.[3] In another well-known lecture, 'Man the Reformer', delivered to an audience of mechanical apprentices, Emerson praises the practical man and method, insisting that without the transformation of the outer world, any attempt to stimulate the intellect would be futile.[4] In his view, man the reformer is at his best when knowledge is applied; only then will his work be truly virtuous and enable or empower him to achieve the higher aims that intellect is striving for. In later essays (such as 'The Young American') Emerson applied his earlier insights to American conditions.[5] The rapidly changing conditions now pose a challenge to the intellect. Only being directly involved with and adjusting to the developments – developments that can be seen in the rising importance of commerce, trade and the development of land – will help the intellect to keep pace with and grow with the changing environment. Such an attitude alone will provide men and women with the opportunity to rise above circumstances and to lead the next generation of Americans to live fulfilling lives. What Emerson argues for is nothing short of a renewed public mind that would guarantee further progress and democracy.

It is but a short step from arguing for a renewed public mind to stressing education as the crucial tool to develop such a public mind. In Emerson's many reflections on the course of American politics this commitment to education stands out.[6] Yet it is also this emphasis on education that becomes a problem – a problem in the sense that the relationship between society and politics is solely defined in educational terms. Education becomes almost a secularised equivalent for the development of the intellect. It is here that the transcendentalist and religious elements in Emerson are still all too obvious – despite being shrouded in secularised language.

To understand how Pragmatism could develop from Emerson, one has to take a closer look at the challenges and intellectual currents of the time following the 'Gilded Age'. The major challenge at the turn of the last century was the accelerating pace of the natural sciences. Against the backdrop of this development, philosophy and social thought seemed to lag behind. In an effort to draw even, Peirce, James and Dewey had to dispose of the philosophical ballast of metaphysics as promoted by Kant and Hegel; they had to throw overboard the European tradition of system-building in philosophy. Against the essentialist European tradition, the pragmatist stressed the empirically oriented side of the process of reflection – the clearest sign of the competition with the natural sciences. Yet to understand these intellectual efforts and the new epistemological paradigm fully, one must also understand why the natural sciences had suddenly become the focus of attention.

Up until the middle of the nineteenth century most American universities were still privately funded and mainly of religious origin. The main subjects of study tended to be theology, morals related to philosophy, and literature and law, all usually taught in the vernacular of the Enlightenment. Yet in a country where the Frontier represented a direct challenge between man and nature, a challenge that had to be overcome by using the intrumental means of technology and industry, the old curricula were neither sufficient nor appropriate in that the new intellectual 'tools' that were now needed were not generated by theology or more secularised, related, disciplines. In an attempt to modernise the curriculum and to open it up to the new demands, state universities were founded. It was in these new universities that the natural sciences and the applied sciences (such as engineering) would begin to flourish. This intellectual environment also explains why a new method of approaching problems had to be 'invented' and why Pragmatism was so drawn to experience and empirical evidence. Pragmatism, in other words, had to leave the ivory tower of philosophy in order to conceptualise and conquer the real, modern world – a world that demanded concrete answers to concrete questions. The early history of Pragmatism and the biographies of its main architects still reflect the way Pragmatism tried to come to terms with the modern American world. C.S. Peirce had been an astronomer at Harvard University before developing his ideas of how to situate the process of scientific discovery. William James, also from Harvard, was more drawn towards psychology – but again, only after years of scientific research and observation which led him to reflect upon the subjective dimensions of the scientific enterprise. John Dewey participated in an educational project linked to the University of Chicago, where he observed the learning process of children, before developing his pedagogical theory and his *Reconstruction in Philosophy*.[7]

Intellectual historians have differing opinions on who qualifies as the first Pragmatist. As has been stressed, Ralph Waldo Emerson can certainly be regarded as a forerunner of Pragmatism, but it is probably appropriate to attribute the label of the first real pragmatist to Charles Sanders Peirce. It was Peirce who first conceived of a theory of meaning and of 'states of belief'. Like other pragmatists, he defined his intellectual efforts less in terms of content and more as 'a method of science in which belief is determined by some external permanency – by something upon which our thinking has no effect'.[8] We can already see from this statement the preoccupation with objectivity and Peirce's attempt to build epistemological investigations in terms similar to the natural sciences. Yet Peirce also recognised philosophical investigation as a human enterprise, an enterprise based on interaction and habit. For this purpose the distinction between true belief (which he saw as a belief in the real) and false belief (which he saw as a belief in fiction) was crucial. Yet if the whole function of thought is to produce habits of action, how are we able to determine which beliefs serve to guide and lead us to the truth? Furthermore, why is true belief essential for the scientific process when false belief is not? The only way to find out, according to Peirce, is to look at the way we interpret the process of discovery and perception itself. It is here that Peirce develops his theory of language and signs. Only if we can make our ideas clear and if we systematically determine what the relationship between our consciousness and the objective world/reality is and what we mean by using a certain language and certain signs to describe the process of discovery and the relationship between observing subject and observed object, can we talk about establishing truth.

As has been stressed, Peirce aims at an epistemological grounding similar to that in the natural sciences, yet at the same time he also dissents from the classical theorising of subject–object relationships that characterised the scientific research: for the first time 'meaning' becomes crucial – and it does so not in abstract philosophical ways but under concrete circumstances. It is exactly this combination of concreteness and meaning that proved to be the crucial legacy of Peirce upon which other pragmatists would elaborate.

Even though Peirce qualifies as the first real pragmatist, he himself did not use the word 'Pragmatism'. 'Pragmatism' as a label became popular only through his Harvard colleague, William James. In one of James' most renowned books, actually entitled *Pragmatism*, he outlines the main objectives of the paradigm.[9] Referring directly to his predecessor, Peirce, James distinguishes between two features in Pragmatism which are both central to its understanding. There is, first of all, the insistence that Pragmatism is a method, a certain way of thinking and of 'making our ideas clear'. Furthermore, the pragmatic method aims at the investigation of concrete, practical consequences of habit or human action; it aims in other words at the explanation of human experiences. Related to this is the second definition or understanding of Pragmatism: instead of aiming at the one truth as in essentialist philosophising, which characterises so much of European thought, Pragmatism uses 'theories . . . (as) instruments, not answers to enigmas in which we can rest'.[10] This focus shifts away from 'first things', principles and 'final results' and aims instead at processes and the underlying 'new' truths, 'fruits, consequences, facts' (James) that need to be revealed.

It is not difficult to decipher the peculiar American dimensions in James' philosophising. As a matter of fact, one could almost understand Pragmatism as modern America's secularised belief system. Was it not the processual dimension that distinguished the errand in the wilderness and the American Jeremiad from the 'static' European belief systems and conditions? Was it not the experience of the flight from Egypt, the exodus that was revived and re-lived on American soil? And was not the Frontier as an institution an incarnation of constant change, of process and progress? To all of this Pragmatism gave a new, more secularised interpretation and explanation. Furthermore, it combined the older political philosophy with liberal and republican ideas. It was this synthesis which explained the ultimate success of pragmatism in the form of one person – John Dewey.

James had paved the way for Dewey by distinguishing the American pragmatists' way of thinking from the rationalist European way. While the pragmatists' reasoning was experience-based and concerned with facts and concreteness, with truth in particular cases, with process, with an American 'world in the making', and finally with truths that specified the good and ultimately led to liberal reform, the European rationalists were unable to recognise the concrete, and dealt with a static, ready-made world, which in turn led to abstractions and to a static notion of correspondence between thought and reality. John Dewey's conceptualisation and reformulation of Pragmatism as a consciously liberal and republican enterprise would elaborate on this form of humanist reasoning first discussed in James; additionally, it would also refer back to Peirce in its emphasis on the proper forms of investigation – however, this time it would not only refer to the scientific process of discovery, but also to the understanding of the social process as a whole.

Out of the many books and essays that John Dewey published during his lifetime *The Public and its Problems*[11] stands out in its attempt to conceptualise the modern social and political process in pragmatist terms. It also stands out because it marks a shift not only from earlier pragmatic focus on scientific inquiries (as in Peirce) and psychological concerns (as in James) to modern social and political processes, but also in terms of a departure from interpreting the American world solely in political terms. Though it is true that other thinkers have tried to understand and explain the modern social world, not least Dewey's colleague from the University of Chicago, George Herbert Mead, it is Dewey, and later Pragmatism, who cut all ties with social theory's Darwinian origins and conceived of the social only in terms of 'the social'.

As has been stressed above, Dewey applies the pragmatic vocabulary in order to understand the modern social world. The distinction between private and public is crucial for this enterprise. Dewey distinguishes between the two concepts not in terms of property but in terms of 'the extent and scope of the consequences of acts'.[12] The very fact that we do not come into being as monads, or Robinson Crusoes, that rather we are socialised and always live connected to and associated with other human beings, makes us social beings who for the most part depend on the public realm. The state, as an association dependent through the wide extent and scope of human action involved in its maintenance, is an institution that in the ideal sense should fully represent the broader articulate social world which Dewey calls the public. Yet, as Dewey tries to show, this is unfortunately not always the case; a situation may arise where 'the public which generated political forms is passing away, but the power and lust of possession remain in the hands of the officers and agencies which the dying public instituted'.[13] To illustrate the contradiction, Dewey refers directly to the American experience. In the beginning there were only small communities, families or clans, maybe a union of families – hence there was no need for a public or a state. The situation only changed once the consequences of action began to transcend the narrow circle of families and friends. New forms of associations became necessary, first a town or county council, later a province, then a state; in the end a confederation of states was called for – as was the case in America. The scope of the chains of action and interaction becomes now larger; rules of law are established in order to channel action; the distinction between private and public becomes more differentiated. A plurality of groups develops, all necessarily interconnected with each other. A division of labour, an 'indefinite overlapping' of individuals, groups and action has been reached. This is what Dewey calls 'society'. But, as he reminds us, society is constructed from many things and many interests. The question therefore arises as to how representative or how democratic a state or its government can be in the light of these plural forms.

Dewey points out that liberalism attempted to give a solution to the problem of democratic government. It highlighted the fear of government; because of the negative experiences with autocratic forms in the past, it saw reduction or minimal government as the solution (and since autocratic forms of government very often appeared in conjunction with an estab-lished ecclesiastical institution, it also argued for explicitly secularised political reform of state and government). To secure life under modern government, liberalism referred to a higher authority – nature and natural rights. Dewey sees it as a strange paradox that while modern man becomes more and more social (interaction-wise, that is), he continues to concep-tualise this experience in terms of individualist attitudes and behaviour, as if modern individuals were liberated from all associations. Furthermore, this thinking eventually led to economic liberalism – a standpoint that regards all individuals as natural human beings, acting out 'beneficent natural laws' (Dewey) on the market. Dewey opposes such a view; he regards such individualistic philosophy as a failed attempt to understand the modern forms of social life. While such an individualistic view might have been appropriate under the conditions which the founding generations experienced in the time of the colonies, where there was almost face-to-face communication and smaller public arenas, such a view becomes dysfunctional under conditions of 'differential wants, purposes and methods' that lead to 'forms of associated action', that are 'so massive and extensive that they determine the most significant constituents of the public and the residence of power' and inevitably 'reach out to grasp the agencies of government' itself.[14]

To be sure, Dewey does not talk about the end of the public, he only states the dangerous contradiction to be found in institutions that had developed out of earlier public forms, as these in most cases are no longer relevant or appropriate under new, modern conditions and would inevitably lead to restricting the volume of the modern public voice. To use an example from Dewey: the town meeting is no longer appropriate in the sense that the people can vote on the measures that will directly affect their lives. The scale of interaction has risen to such a height that even the federal government is short of answers: 'the public seems to be lost . . . the government, officials and their activities, are plainly with us . . . but where is the public which these officials are supposed to represent?'[15] Dewey quotes from a periodical to highlight the ultimate state that had been reached: 'Since the end of the Civil War practically all the more important measures which have been embodied in federal legislation have been reached without a national election which turned upon the issue and which divided the two major parties.'[16] To be sure, many small communities do exist, but they do not form a 'Great Community' with a functioning public.

But how can what has been said be linked to what Peirce and James saw as essential? Why, after all, is a functioning public so important to Dewey? The answer to these questions is simple: it is only through communication that we can give meaning to things. The idea of the public is crucial in this respect; only if we have the appropriate means can we communicate our modern experiences. The current state of affairs is a far cry from that. As Dewey points out, it is a Babel, but it is a Babel not 'of tongues but of the signs and symbols without which shared experience is impossible'.[17] Dewey does not say that we are not living in a democratic state, his point is rather that democracy hasn't lived up to its promises. If it is true that democracy is 'the idea of community life itself',[18] then a framework – a larger public – must be found under which we can share those experiences, in particular those that no longer stem from face-to-face communication in small communities and publics. Today each citizen is part of a national web of communication, but at the same time this citizen does not feel positive about being part of such a web – mainly due to the fact that there are no common signs and symbols. One could describe the state of the public in almost Hegelian terms: the larger public exists in itself but it does not live for itself. At this point, Peirce and James' arguments are directly relevant. As there is no reciprocal give and take in this public, we cannot agree on what the facts are – hence no knowledge can develop. Habit certainly exists, but it is a habit in which thinking remains underdeveloped or follows the division of labour where thinking is only to be found among scientists and intellectuals. Where no democratic thinking habits exist, no social knowledge can develop, conditions cannot be controlled or, again, follow the intellectual division of labour. It is this last scenario that Pragmatism abhors. Useful knowledge can only come into being through ideas being continually challenged through practice. For this purpose a public framework where dissemination and communication lead to public opinion, which then leads to judgement, is the *conditio sine qua non*. In the ideal sense such a public would lead to continuous inquiry – this time not only for the purpose of generating scientific knowledge but to the benefit of the social fabric as a whole.[19]

The beginning of this chapter stressed that form is condensed content and within this chapter it is demonstrated that Pragmatism in particular serves as its perfect example. Yet it would be wrong to reduce Pragmatism solely to questions of methods and forms of inquiry. As we have seen with Dewey, Pragmatism also leads us away from perceiving American society and politics only in terms of 'the political'. With Dewey a radical paradigm change occurs: 'the social' can no longer be neglected; and as will be seen in further chapters, the discovery of 'the social' is the necessary precondition to discuss such issues as 'power and democracy', 'justice and injustice', 'multiculturalism and pluralism', 'civil society, social theory and the task of intellectuals', and the general state American public philosophy is in.

With the rise of the social sciences in conjunction with the expansion of higher education, the intellectual Jeremiad in the form of Pragmatist thinking gained a firmer and more solid basis from which to understand, judge and criticise American society. But even this critique – though now having a firm base in the humanities and the social sciences – remained within the limits of the Jeremiadan discourse described earlier by Bercovitch. What did change though was the language; it developed into a more secularised, sócial language. This is particularly true for two thinkers who are firmly rooted in the Pragmatist tradition, Thorstein Veblen and C. Wright Mills. Both can be regarded as outstanding examples of a more sociologically refined critique.

Thorstein Veblen's work, which was not only influenced by American Pragmatism and critical economics but also by Social Darwinism, set the agenda and tone for the future refined development of the Pragmatist Jeremiad. The 'American Marx', as he was called, formulated a critique of American institutions that was unique in its specificity and concreteness.[20] Veblen really took issue with the time he lived in: the Gilded Age was a time of unregulated growth, as capitalism expanded into every corner of the North American continent. As Veblen shows, the country town and the independent farmer were replaced by the city and the new captains of industry. Agriculture became mechanised. As a result of this, people were liberated, leaving the rural environment to try their luck in the rapidly developing cities. These people moved into new, mostly unskilled, jobs that an expanding, urban-environment industry offered to them. In the factories and mass-production plants another modernisation process was already under way. In particular, the sphere of immediate production provided insights into radical changes. Here, a rationalising process was under way that changed the traditional patterns of work: craftsmanship, the state of industrial art and the captains of industry were replaced with paper shufflers, 'coupon clippers' and, finally, the captain of solvency. The latter type was, as Veblen critically observes, no longer familiar with shop-floor activities; rather he made his fortune focusing on separate activities such as negotiations, investment and banking. In the eyes of the critical Social Darwinist Veblen, the captain of solvency and the economic institution he represented were no longer fit for survival. According to Veblen, an obvious sign of the decline was the fact that they had formed a new leisure class that found its ultimate expression in conspicuous consumption. For the first time in America an elite had developed that no longer followed the Protestant work ethic, and no longer represented the self-made man or the 'enterprising entrepreneur'; rather America expressed herself now solely in terms of pecuniary culture. As Veblen points out, such a development also found an equivalent and expression in higher education and intellectual activity. The result was that the critical dimension got lost – as Veblen shows particularly in his field, the realm of economics. Economics as an academic subject was no longer taught as an evolutionary science, but rather as a 'hands-on', taxing activity where most people did not realise what they were doing, where they were coming from, or what overall purpose economics should serve. Instead, economic activity had become an end in itself.

It was left to the maverick and muckraking sociologist C. Wright Mills to take Veblen's critique one step further. Whereas Veblen took particular issue with economic institutions, Mills focused on the political sociology of the United States. In particular his trilogy on the American power structure revealed how far America had developed from the earlier promise of political and social equality.[21] The American working class was a far cry from Marx's promise of the revolutionary 'universalist' – oriented class. Mills showed that the 'working class' organisations and representatives were by no means prepared to speak out for and act in the name of the masses of blue-collar employees. Instead, the labour leaders followed their own particularistic and self-serving ends. The newly emerged middle class was in an even worse position. Forming a 'pyramid within a pyramid' (Mills), its top stratum looked up to the still further top of the overall social hierarchy; at the same time the mass of white collar workers faced the threat of sinking and getting closer to the bottom of the social scale. Experiencing alienation while at the same time being less organised and less class-conscious – in short atomistic and apathetic individuals – this new middle class was even less of a hope in terms of social and political emancipation than the organised working class was. In ironic contrast to Marx's predictions, Mills encountered a real class-consciousness only among the tripartite power elite (consisting of the military, the political directorate and the corporate rich). This power elite had come into being with the New Deal and had managed to stay in power with the somewhat artificial help of World War II and the Cold War. Mills stressed that this new American power elite only could have become so powerful because of the apathy of modern mass society and the erosion of the American publics. This was shocking news indeed. Mills' modern Jeremiad revealed that the promise and the dream of America had turned into an institutional nightmare – a nightmare that was no longer limited to individual failure but had been triggered and was now pursued with the help of socially and politically 'organised irresponsibility'.[22] The only way out of this dilemma would be the re-establishment of a functioning public sphere which Mills called the 'cultural apparatus'. Within this cultural apparatus a new, secularised priesthood tried to pursue the American dream. Public intellectuals or 'cultural workers' (whose work consists mainly of dealing with symbols), would speak out and fight against the distortion of the American dream in which unequal and undemocratic institutional 'history making' had prevailed. In Mills' concrete Utopia they would use their unique intellect as a means for gaining back the power for every individual to make history, to 'democratise history making'.

This form of pursuing American ends with genuinely American means must clearly be regarded as the most secularised form of the Jeremiad. In modernising the Jeremiad, Mills indeed came close to his predecessor Veblen, about whom he once commented that 'his criticism of institutions and the personnel of American society was based without exception upon the belief that they did not adequately fulfil American values. If he was, as I believe, a Socratic figure, he was in his own way as American as Socrates in his way was Athenian. As a critic, Veblen was effective precisely because he used American values to criticise American reality. He merely took these values seriously and used them with devastating rigour'.[23]

Notes

1. The second 'wave' of Pragmatism, associated with names such as Richard Rorty and Hilary Putnam, only developed much later and in a different context, and is therefore not dealt with in this chapter.
2. Ralph Waldo Emerson: *Essays and Lectures* (New York: The Library of America 1983).
3. 'The American Scholar' in: ibid. pp. 51–71.
4. 'Man the Reformer' in: ibid. pp. 133–50.
5. 'The Young American' in: ibid. pp. 211–30.
6. Representative in this respect is his essay 'Politics' in: ibid. pp. 559–71. For the role of the public see Emerson's essay on 'Culture' in: ibid. pp. 1015–34.
7. *Reconstruction in Philosophy* (New York: Henry Holt and Company 1921/revised edition: Boston: Beacon Press 1948).
8. Quoted after an editorial comment by Russel B. Goodman in his *Pragmatism – A Contemporary Reader* (New York/London: Routledge 1995) p. 35.
9. William James: *Pragmatism – A New Name for Some Old Ways of Thinking* (New York/London 1907). Parts of this book are reprinted in John J. McDermott (ed.) *The Writings of William James* (Chicago/London: The University of Chicago Press 1977).
10. *Pragmatism – A Contemporary Reader*, p. 56.
11. *The Public and its Problems* (New York: Henry Holt and Company 1927).
12. Ibid. p. 15.
13. Ibid. p. 31.
14. Ibid. pp. 103 and 107.
15. Ibid. p. 116f.
16. Ibid. p. 120.
17. Ibid. p. 142.
18. Ibid. p. 148.
19. It was left to another pragmatist, George Herbert Mead, to elaborate on this. Mead's contribution led to the development of an entire new branch of sociology – the study of symbolic interaction.

20. Thorstein Veblen: *The Theory of the Leisure Class* (New York 1899); *The Instinct of Workmanship* (New York: Macmillan 1914), and *Absentee Ownership and Business Enterprise in Recent Times – The Case of America* (New York: Viking Press 1923). *The Portable Veblen* (ed. Max Lerner; New York: Viking Press 1948) is useful in its collection of texts that are otherwise difficult to find.

21. C. Wright Mills: *The New Man of Power* (New York: Harcourt, Brace and Company 1948); *White Collar* (New York/Oxford: Oxford University Press 1951) and *The Power Elite* (New York/Oxford: Oxford University Press 1956).

22. See Mills' collection of politically inspired essays in: C. Wright Mills (Irving Louis Horowitz, ed.): *Power, Politics and People* (New York/Oxford: Oxford University Press 1963).

23. C. Wright Mills: Introduction to the Mentor Edition of Thorstein Veblen: *The Theory of The Leisure Class* (New York: The New American Library 1953), p. 14ff.

Part II

Theorising the Social:
Modern Applications of American Social
and Political Thought

Chapter 6

Democracy and Power

Barrington Moore's distinction between dictatorship and democracy as two different paths leading to modernity ● Moore's further distinction between different Western paths leading to democracy: the English, French and American cases in comparison ● From agriculture to industry: discussing the results of transitional experiences ● Successful models come to terms with social inequality ● Investigating emerging power structures: masses and elites ● C. Wright Mills' description of the power elite – Robert A. Dahl's response to Mills: the American hybrid model of democracy ● Democratising democracy through deliberation; Amy Gutmann and Dennis Thompson's reflections on moral disagreement ● Other contributions to the idea of deliberative democracy: theorising difference

The relationship between democracy and power is a precarious one. In what follows, a three-step argument concerning this tenuous relationship will be set out. We will look first at what distinguishes American democracy from dictatorship and second at what distinguishes it from other democracies. In this context we will pick out as a central theme the historical relationship between capitalism and democracy in America and we will look at the internal contradictions of American democracy – particularly the relationship between the normative dimension of democracy as 'rule of the people' and the contradictory reality of the existence of elites. Finally, contemporary conceptions of democracy will be discussed. Of particular importance will be conceptions of American democracy which are supposed to mediate between the normative dimensions and the reality of American democracy.

In order to determine what distinguishes America's path to modernity from others, a comparative view is needed. Within the social sciences, Barrington Moore's study of the *Social Origins of Dictatorship and Democracy* ranks as a modern classic within the field of comparative studies.[1] In particular, Moore's study aims at an international comparison on at least two levels: first, the distinction between dictatorship and democracy as two very different paths leading to modernity; and second, the further distinction and differentiation between the English, the French and the American ways to capitalist democracy.

According to Moore, there are three routes to modernity: the path of bourgeois revolution leading to capitalist democracy (as can be observed in the cases of England, France and the USA); the path of capitalism without democracy, leading to fascism (the cases of Germany and Japan); and finally, the road that leads to communism without democracy, to be found particularly in countries where agrarian societies had to provide an answer to widespread agrarian unrest (the cases of the Soviet Union and China). In the early cases of bourgeois revolution, the English Puritan Revolution, the French Revolution and the American Civil War created a constellation where both the land-owning upper class and the peasants became either part of the capitalist and democratic process of innovation or were completely eradicated by the new development. The German and Japanese cases of capitalism without democracy differed in that the impulse and impact of the bourgeoisie turned out to be weaker. In their attempt to provide an answer to modern capitalism, the German and Japanese bourgeoisie suppressed the revolutionary social movements from below and instead initiated a 'revolution from above', led by a new coalition in which the land-owning classes continued to play a role. While this coalition could eventually function as a catalyst for industrial capitalist development, it had detrimental political results in that democratic reforms were rendered impossible. In the case of Russia (including the later Soviet Union) and China, that is communism without democracy, the situation was equally disadvantageous. Here, the civic urban element was even weaker than in the case of Germany and Japan; at the same time there were too many peasants; on top of this, the large agrarian bureaucracies prevented any innovation. Taken together these circumstances explain why a comparable industrial infrastructure could not develop and why only enforced industrialisation could take place. Still, an answer had to be found in order to cope with rising inequality and the radical demand for social justice; eventually 'actually existing communism' provided the answer. As this brief description of the different paths to modernity shows, America belonged to the countries which would allow it to be set on a formidable road to capitalist democracy. What still demands an explanation though is the unique path that distinguishes the United States from other paths to capitalist democracy – particularly those of Western Europe.

According to Moore, societies bound for the democratic process learn from each other. In the never-ending search for democracy three features in particular are outstanding:

1. The decision to stand up against arbitrary rule.
2. The replacement of arbitrary systems with rational and legitimate forms of power and coercion.
3. The guarantee of the widest possible participation in the decision-making processes.

Over the course of the last four centuries England, France and the United States have gone through different historical constellations, yet the net outcome has been those prevailing features described above. In order to find out how this was achieved it is necessary to follow Moore's next step of historical comparison – the comparison of those countries that followed the democratic capitalist path.

For Moore, the decisive factor that set England on the road to democracy was what he calls 'the Puritan Revolution'. The attribute 'puritan' is used mainly because the social struggle that took place in the English countryside took on the specific form of a struggle between differing religious convictions and factions. To be more precise, the struggle about the commercial value of landed property must be understood as a struggle between the aristocracy (which later became the landed gentry) and the peasantry; it was a struggle under the eyes of a comparatively weak monarchy that was far from exercising absolute power. All the factions involved also had deep religious affiliations – hence the specific form of the conflict where the 'materialist' interest is entwined with the 'cultural' or 'religious superstructure'. The struggle intensified with increasing commercial trade in the cities and with a growing market in the countryside. Both movements eventually paved the way for the development of capitalist agriculture. The social struggle finally turned into a struggle over political control and led to political revolution. Moore stresses that it is very hard to identify clear-cut class boundaries in the course of the English Revolution; also the result of the English Civil War was not a radical shift in terms of property relations; furthermore, particularly with restoration, it became clear that in terms of long-term results the revolution did not provide a radical change in terms of political power shifts. Yet it would be wrong to assume that the Puritan Revolution had no results at all. Moore stresses that in England it paved the way for an alliance consisting of a land-owning gentry whose interests overlapped with those of the emerging urban bourgeoisie. It was the victory of this constellation that created the long-lasting alliance between parliamentary democracy and capitalism. To summarise then, because the land-owning aristocracy saw the new possibilities and advantages in capitalism, it became an agent of change and limited political reform – and thus was not swept away by other historical forces. The long-term losers were of course the peasantry, which under the conditions of capitalist agriculture was slowly eroded – paving the way for the creation of the working class. Moore sees the genuine English contribution to the development of capitalist democracy as that change was mediated. After the English Revolution, coercion and capitalist hegemony were given a chance to develop relatively peacefully in the form of law and order. England thus entered modern times as a capitalist democracy with no significant peasant problem, with a majority of the population seeing its main economic base in capitalist production, and with a relatively strong parliamentary tradition which would guarantee liberty and the rule of law – all three factors contributing to what can be called 'controlled change'.

The case of France differed from the English one, not least because of different class constellations prior to the French Revolution. The French aristocracy, unlike the English one, was closer to the monarch. In France there was not the relatively independently-minded aristocracy with an interest in the value of propertied land and an emerging capitalist agriculture as in England, but rather there was an aristocracy which lived directly off the surplus created by a peasantry which worked the land and was bound to the aristocracy through a complex relationship consisting of feudal bonds and inferior status. The interest of the French aristocracy was one of immediate gain in that it tried to generate more output from the peasantry – mainly through using the political means of state and law. It is this constellation, a situation where surplus is guaranteed through the close relationship between aristocracy, the state and the legal estate, which created the social discontent that would lead to the French Revolution. Thus, in France commercial influences did not lead to gradual erosion and final abolition of feudal structures, as they did in England, but rather they led to increased tension. The emerging bourgeoisie, which saw no way to success other than buying titles and thereby gaining access to the aristocracy, questioned why it should continue to buy titles, thus questioning the entire social and political framework. The peasantry also wondered why title and privilege alone qualified one to enter the ranks of money-makers, why their lot in life was restricted to working the land. It was the combined efforts of both the bourgeoisie and the peasantry together with the impact of crucial revolutionary events, which explains the radical turn and outcome of the French Revolution – namely the final abolition of all feudal remnants. Yet, as Moore notes, it was also the tension between the city (in particular Paris) and the countryside (almost the entire rest of the country) that helps to explain some of the more devastating results of the Revolution, particularly the violence and the terror.

To summarise then, the French Revolution put an end to the 'feudalisation' of the bourgeoisie. But prior to the Revolution and in contrast to

England the bourgeoisie did not become part of the democratisation process, but instead needed a few more decades of 'collaboration' with the Crown before it could finally abolish the institutions that had blocked its path. In this struggle the radicalisation of the countryside played a major role, but also posed new problems in that it created a kind of 'second front' or, as Moore calls it, a second revolution – a revolution that proved to be a major obstacle in the political and social success of the bourgeoisie. In the end, the French Revolution proved to be a major breakthrough only in so far as it led to the abolition of a feudalist remnant past and in preparing the ground for fully-fledged capitalism.

As has been pointed out by other authors, the situation was very different in America; there was no monarch, no land-owning aristocracy and no homogeneous and compact peasantry. Yet the fact that a European-like constellation was absent does not mean that the development of capitalist democracy was made impossible. As Moore stresses, it was indeed possible for capitalist democracy to develop in America; yet we do not fully understand its history if we focus too much on the War of Independence. Moore's genuine contribution consists of the insistence that it was only later, with the American Civil War, that we can speak of a fundamental change within American society. Two things were of particular relevance: first, it was the Civil War which separated the agricultural from the industrial epoch in American history and which put America on the road to capitalism; second, it was thus the Civil War which, in essence led to democracy in America.

To appreciate how this was possible, one has to understand the three different types of society that existed in the middle of the nineteenth century: the South with its cotton plantations, the West as a settlement of free farmers and the Northeast, where industrial development had progressed further than anywhere else within United States territory. Eventually trade and communication between the North East and the West improved; individualistic small-scale capitalism became popular among farmers in the West – not least due to the demand from the East which turned farming into a commercial enterprise. It was then that the South alone stood out in its specific mode of production of cotton based on slavery – against a coalition of 'steel and barley' modernisers. In contrast to Europe, where the revolutionary force consisted of a coalition made up of non-reactionary land-owning aristocrats, in the United States free farmers in a progressive alliance with industrial entrepreneurs formed the successful coalition. Particularly in respect of the development in the West and concerning the relationship between capitalists and workers in the North East, one precondition in particular proved to be crucial: that of the availability of land. It was this precondition which provided the necessary geographical space – space that was crucial for the new formation of classes and which in the long run prevented a reactionary or conservative solution to capitalism's challenge. If this interpretation is accepted, then the American Civil War was in fact not solely a struggle as to which of two different forms of society and civilisation should be supported by the federal government – a society based on free labour or a society based on enslaved labour. As Moore stresses, as a result of the Civil War America rejected the Southern civilisation; at a certain stage in capitalism's development it became simply dysfunctional; and the model of capitalist democratic competition was favoured in its place. As Moore sees it, the abolition of slavery created the political conditions under which capitalism could thrive.

If one had to summarise Barrington Moore's epistemological interest and his analysis, it would be apt to say that his main preoccupation is with undifferentiated ideas of equality. In the transitional period from agriculture to industry, the idea of social equality, not freedom, became the crucial question for the beleaguered peasants; indeed they argued for freedom in terms of equality. The successful transition to capitalist democracy only occurred where and when some aspect of this demand was fulfilled – hence the formation of capitalist democracy in England, France and the United States. Within these countries, which had realised a successful transition, the United States stands out again because it lacked the fetters of the past that bound England and France. Being a latecomer, the United States was in a position to learn from the mistakes of the European past; it is exactly this position which allowed it to balance capitalism and democracy better than any of its predecessors.

It is through Barrington Moore's comparative analysis that we begin to understand how capitalism evolved in the United States. It still remains open, however, how a balance between capitalism and democracy can be maintained. What exactly is the relationship between political equality (as promised by democracy) and social inequality (as generated by capitalism)? How can we speak of a democracy when we know of the existence of a power elite? In order to find an answer to these questions, one must engage in the discussions of how power is distributed and legitimised in present-day America.

Among the many discussions the one triggered by C. Wright Mills' groundbreaking book *The Power Elite* stands out in particular.[2] The leading question that Mills is concerned with is how, and under which modern conditions, do people with different class and status backgrounds make history? Mills' answer to this question is a differentiated one: Among the modern twentieth-century labour class, it is only a tiny part of the organised labour movement, that is the higher union representatives who are in a position to make history. Mills is even more pessimistic in his judgement on the new middle class; as dependent working employees they are exposed to the modern forms of alienation without having the class-consciousness and the force to unionise that the working class has. Only in the case of the higher circles, a tripartite power elite recruited from the political, economic and military realms of American society, does Mills recognise a homogeneous class conscientious enough to make history in the emphatic sense of the word. The very existence of such a power elite, of people who are in a position to be 'more equal' to make history more than others, contradicts the normative values of any notion of democracy. One must therefore question what precisely were and remain the concrete conditions for the existence of an American power elite? In answering this question, one first must discuss the general presuppositions of Mills' approach. Two assumptions are at the heart of Mills' argument: first, the concept of power as proposed by Max Weber, which suggests that power is the competence to pursue one's own interests, even against the will of others, and second that power can take shape in many ways, but to be and to remain stable it needs an institutional form. The question that follows from these general presuppositions is: how did America develop to a point where such a power elite could emerge? In Europe wealth, power and prestige were clearly separated along class lines; in America, as Barrington Moore has stressed, the situation was different; there were no such distinctions along class lines. The very lack of conflict between two opposed forces might serve to explain why at a later stage in history the American power elite was able to combine all three features in one – wealth, power, and prestige. Mills also hints at another reason why the American power elite was able to become so successful: from the beginning the American power elite had been on 'the right side of history' – a factor that has been stressed by Louis Hartz. Yet all this should not lead us to assume that the power elite was something that developed 'naturally' and remained unchanged. As Mills points out, we can distinguish between various stages in the development of America's power elite. From the time of the American Revolution until the end of President John Adams' term in office the economic, political and military institutions were one undifferentiated unit; there was in other words no institutional power to speak of. Rather, power was exercised by and limited to a few outstanding individuals. The second phase, roughly covering the early nineteenth century, saw an adjustment of the economic, political and military spheres of economy in an expanding and ever increasing territory. A result of this was the formation of various decentralised, scattered local and regional elite circles. This second phase was also marked by the rise and increased importance of the economic sphere. The third phase began with the division and further differentiation of northern and southern states. The Civil War led to a further rise and empowerment of economic and industrial institutions; a result was the creation of big trusts that eventually became more powerful than the political institutions. The economic elite became stronger than the political elite until the balance began to be re-addressed by the re-emergence of the political elite – represented and symbolised by the increasing power of the presidency. The fourth phase, at the turn of the century, sees the development of new power structures within the economic and military realms. The power of the old capitalists and old political elites came to an end with the world economic crisis and a new generation gained access to the higher circles. The reshuffling led to a power shift – with the political realm taking the initiative and gaining hegemony. The Second World War obviously granted the military more status, and towards the war's end the fifth phase of development of America's power elite began. The alliance between business and politics had become obvious, creating the infrastructure of what would eventually be known as the military-industrial complex. However, the convergence of economic, political and military interests only became fully developed after World War II and particularly during the Cold War. The power elite that Mills described during the time he wrote (1956) was now a tripartite elite that, despite its internally differentiated recruiting processes, was much more homogeneous than any of its predecessors – not least due to the fact that its power was built on the back of institutions.

Mills acknowledges that such a powerful elite had become possible not only because its power was based on the rising importance of institutions and their control, but also because America no longer provided a public infrastructure in which the further progress of American society could be discussed and decided upon. The lack of genuine public and democratic discourse led to the creation of a mass society where the blue-and white-collar workers formed the passive mass at the bottom of the pyramid of power, one which was in no position to have a say in the decisions which had an impact on their lives; on the other hand, at the top of the power pyramid, a small group of the elite which in essence determined the course of history. In short, America had been radically transformed from a democracy where the people made public decisions that had an impact on them, to a formal democracy in which power was no longer in the hands of the masses but rather rested with a powerful oligarchy.

Mills' heretical and radical view of the state of modern American society did not, however, go unchallenged. In particular, Robert A. Dahl challenged Mills' views from what can be called a 'pluralist' standpoint.

In two books, the theoretical work *A Preface to Democratic Theory* and the more empirically oriented work *Who Governs?*, he maintains that power and democracy in twentieth-century America are the products of an American hybrid, a political system that functions normally in that it creates elites, but which is still flexible and decentralised enough to allow any significant group to be heard effectively and to influence the decision-making process.[3] To prove his point, Dahl discusses, first, three models of democracy in his *A Preface to Democratic Theory*, before dealing with the 'American hybrid'. The American hybrid is then tested empirically in the study of his home town of New Haven. The three other democratic theories which Dahl discusses and which he sees as relevant to the American experience are Madisonian democracy, populist democracy and polyarchal democracy. Each model has its advantages and shortcomings. The Madisonian notion of democracy must be understood as a model that favours a compromise between the power of both the majority and minority in order to avoid a non-tyrannical republic. It must be understood as an attempt to balance 'the political equality of all adult citizens on the one side, and the desire to limit their sovereignty on the other'.[4] The problem with Madisonian democracy, however, lies in its many unspoken presuppositions and premises to achieve practically the compromise between the equal rights of the many and the liberties of minorities of certain status, power and/or wealth. The older notion of populistic democracy – which also found expression in America – clearly stands in contrast to the Madisonian model. Although in theory populist democracy favours political equality, popular sovereignty and majority rule, in practice it also tries to restrain the power of the majority – particularly when one reflects on the empirical fact that in each society a ruling class develops over time. The central question that remains then is how can one realistically demand equality and from whom? Should one hand back the controlling powers to society and depend on voluntary self-restraint, or should one favour institutional security mechanisms, such as the Supreme Court? Dahl merely raises the question and thus hints at a serious problem of democratic theory; at the same time he cannot provide a direct answer. The third model that Dahl discusses is polyarchal democracy. This model consists of a complex descriptive procedure: it looks at various forms of social organisations and tries to identify those patterns which favour democratic arrangements and participation. The problem with such a model is that it has to look at such a variety of circumstances and experiences that its proposals in the end become either chaotic or meaningless when applying it to a particular case such as America.

Out of the strengths and weaknesses of the three models discussed, Dahl suggests that in practice American democracy has both incorporated and rejected parts of the three suggested models. Through its practice of more than 200 years, American democracy realised that it had to come to terms with the various aspects of equality, diversity and intensity of the political process and what it can realistically demand from its active and passive citizens. The outcome has been no small achievement. According to Dahl, the American hybrid model still allows any significant voice, even if it is small, some say and participation in the decision-making process. It is a dynamic, mainly decentralised, system where decisions are being made in an endless bargaining process. Dahl maintains further that, as long as the social preconditions are still in order, this model will survive through 'reinforcing agreement, encouraging moderation and maintaining social peace'.[5]

To prove his point, Dahl elaborated on this assumption by conducting his famous empirical study which dealt with the decision-making process in New Haven. The result of this study showed again that Mills' assumption about the distribution of power was not correct. It is not the power elite or a gigantic bureaucratic machine in Washington DC which decided local political issues, but New Haven's own elected citizens. In opposition to Mills' thesis, Dahl even identifies more self-determination than ever before: while in the old days local oligarchies determined the outcome of local politics, a more democratic form of local government has replaced these traditional elites.

To summarise then, Mills' and Dahl's accounts are in direct opposition. While Mills focuses on the increasing centralisation of political power, Dahl suggests a change of paradigm in looking at local political processes which in his view have not been eroded but which in contrast have become more democratic over time. But there is also the possibility of seeing both views as two sides of the same coin. Perhaps American democracy is schizophrenic in that both centrifugal and decentralising forces are at work. Any further interpretation must also highlight the unresolved tensions that exist between more normative and more descriptive lines of reasoning. Seen in this light, C. Wright Mills could be said to represent the former, while Robert A. Dahl represents the latter. However, both statements must be read as interpretations and representations of the times: maybe America really stood at the crossroads when Mills and Dahl were writing – with one signpost saying 'toward centralisation/power elite' and the other sign hinting 'toward further democratisation'.

As we approach the end of the century new attempts have been made to synthesise the American experience and to balance the theory and practice of American democracy. The most recent attempt to conceptualise democracy – united under the label of 'deliberative democracy' – does not consist of one school of reasoning, but rather gathers together thinkers from different backgrounds. The project of deliberative democracy must be understood as an international effort to theorise the post-1989 world. Not only did we observe the end of communism with the fall of the Berlin Wall, we must not forget either the earlier transitions from dictatorship to democracy in the decade preceding the events of 1989 (particularly in Latin America). This victory of democracy had a wider impact and also influenced the discussion in countries where democracy had already been in place – particularly the United States. Here, democratic theorists again became aware that democracy was not just something static, or a fixed set of procedures, but rather contained a dynamic element, open to changing political and social influences.

In the discussion of Mills' and Dahl's theses one can already identify a tendency towards differentiation – the power elite and decentralisation being just two extreme results of the differentiation process. Clearly, not only the events of 1989 and the preceding 'democratic decade' show that modern systems have to come to terms with even further differentiation, particularly with questions of difference and identity; also 'actually existing democracies' like the United States must do so. Having said that, countries with a long democratic tradition like the United States have the clear advantage over countries where the democratic process is just about to start: democratic procedures are already in place, the rule of law applies, and institutionalised security mechanisms put the stakes high for violations of civil liberties and human rights. Still, countries like the United States are not conflict-free and have to find a democratic answer to internal differentiation as expressed in the insistence of difference and identity.

One of the most challenging attempts to theorise these conflicts has been the 'deliberative democracy' approach of Amy Gutmann and Dennis Thompson.[6] Gutmann and Thompson do not reject procedural republican or constitutional liberal conceptions of democracy; however, they do question the reach or spectrum of these classical conceptions of democracy. In their view, modern American civil society is becoming more and more differentiated, and with differentiation inevitably comes increased tension and conflict – usually based on moral disagreement. The authors are interested in what holds or binds society together in terms of both means and ends. For them the 'ends' is surely the idea of 'the good society', a society that is aware of its citizens' moral agreements and disagreements. Yet their approach is by no means ends-centred; they regard as equally important the relationship of means towards the ends; in other words, at the very end of each agreement or disagreements we find a process (leading up to such an end). The core argument of Gutmann and Thompson is that this process is more likely to have a good end (in the sense that we mutually agree or disagree, yet respect the final outcome) if some form of deliberation has been employed. In their attempt to spell out the conditions of successful deliberation, the authors establish that a good outcome is more likely if certain conditions are met. There are three principles that Gutmann and Thompson regard as essential. Reciprocity helps to regulate public reason; it aims at a balanced relationship in the sense of mutual acknowledgement, respect and integrity, and open-mindedness. Publicity is needed to ensure that arguments can be dealt with openly and in terms of accessibility. Accountability ensures that the division of labour (for example, between representatives and the electorate) doesn't go too far; it aims at a fair balance of '*who* gives the reasons' and to '*whom* reasons should be given'.[7] Three other conditions are in support of these principles: basic liberty ensures that neither paternalist nor moralist values can prevail absolutely. Yet what this entails actually when it comes down to detailed considerations and applications remains open in Gutmann's and Thompson's approach. What they do state, however, is that basic liberty is best assured in a deliberative process when 'citizens begin by asking what policy best enhances personal integrity'.[8] Basic opportunity is another requirement, but again – as in the case of basic liberty – the problems lie in the details; so whether one opts for welfare and under which obligations must be left to detailed discussion. Having said that, to provide citizens with the necessary prerequisites for liberation is absolutely essential. Equal citizenship can thus imply considerable transactions to improve the situation of the not-so-well-off citizens. How far these transactions should go is indeed the question and the discussion in the last of Gutmann and Thompson's requirements – fair opportunity. The authors both favour fair opportunity models, yet also see the problems such programmes have brought in the past. With particular reference to affirmative action programmes that were employed in the past, they state what advantages more deliberation would bring: 'A deliberative perspective leaves more scope for reasonable disagreement than either conventional liberal or egalitarian interpretations of preferential hiring admit, and therefore more scope for wider differences in employment policies than the conventional views suppose. But this perspective also imposes on citizens a greater obligation to account for their choice of policy than they usually assume.'[9]

   To sum up, Gutmann and Thompson have not delivered a 'grand theory' of deliberation. As a matter of fact, as the authors admit, such a theory is impossible. Yet the deliberative approach has widely contributed to the rethinking of democratic arrangements. First, it has hinted at a considerable 'deliberation gap' in existing democracies; second, it has made a contribution towards closing this gap, and finally has attempted to bring norm and practice in modern American civil society closer to each other. Further-more, the 'deliberative democracy' approach has hinted at the danger of an overdevelopment of the division of labour: there is, after all, no special arena where moral reasoning takes place and by no means should deliberation be left only to government. If there is any realm where deliberation could be 'tested out', then it can only be in the educational sphere – in schools, colleges and universities. It is here that citizens can learn that deliberation is 'at the center of everyday politics' (Gutmann and Thompson).

Gutmann and Thompson's account has been the most ambitious attempt to understand and explain deliberative processes; yet there is more to be said about the fuzzy paradigm of deliberative democracy. Let us recount some other prospects within this approach: as has been stated already in Gutmann and Thompson's study, the older republican model underlined the im-portance of ethical foundations through emphasising the pursuit of the 'common good', whereas the liberal model of democracy attempts to mediate the diverting interests of civil society and channel them into workable politics. In contrast, the deliberative model rests on the assump-tion of a 'decentralised society' (Benhabib) based on difference and complex identity formation processes in which the political system is not something that stands 'above' society. As a consequence, a crucial factor in deliberative democracy-based theories' attempts to conceptualise modern democracy is the revival or extension of the public sphere – a thought that had earlier been expressed by Pragmatism's most eloquent thinker John Dewey. Not only would a revitalised public sphere express the dynamics of a modern differentiated society; it would also lead to further democratisation in that power would be checked and controlled and chances to participate in relevant decision-making processes would be enhanced. This then is the common factor of deliberative democracy; but apart from this shared interest in the revival of the public sphere, theorists differ and disagree widely. While the political scientist Sheldon Wolin reminds us that democracy and 'the political' refer to crucial singular experiences that are 'doomed to succeed only temporarily' but that also are 'a recurrent possibility as long as the memory of the political survives',[10] Seyla Benhabib, in her attempt to link the project of deliberative democracy to Habermasian discourse practices, goes so far as to emphasise that the public sphere will actually replace the model that the deliberative assembly found in earlier (republican and liberal) theory.[11] Benjamin Barber goes a step further even. While Benhabib still holds on to the idea of communicative reason, Barber in his neo-republican but surprisingly pragmatic view of strong democracy holds that reason is only part of 'being reasonable about the democratic procedure' and no longer part of the content of democracy.[12] In his view, citizens are active 24-hour citizens; with the help of the modern means of communication they can participate in all the decisions that have an impact on them. Finally here is a model that also demonstrates the weakness of the deliberative view of democracy; in its attempt to overcome the classic liberal and republican views of democracy, it has created – against all good intentions – an Orwellian, totalitarian citizen who is able to participate and decide all the time – however, what he or she decides upon is no longer that clear: the normative element has outflanked realism.

Notes

1. Barrington Moore Jr: *Social Origins of Dictatorship and Democracy* (Boston: Beacon Press 1966).
2. C. Wright Mills: *The Power Elite* (New York/Oxford: Oxford University Press 1956).
3. Robert A. Dahl: *A Preface to Democratic Theory* (Chicago/London: University of Chicago Press 1956). *Who Governs?* (New Haven/London: Yale University Press 1961).
4. *A Preface to Democratic Theory*, p. 4.
5. Ibid. p. 151.
6. Amy Gutmann and Dennis Thompson: *Democracy and Disagreement* (Cambridge, MA: The Belknap Press of Harvard University Press 1996).
7. Ibid. p. 128.
8. Ibid. p. 272.
9. Ibid. p. 345.
10. Sheldon Wolin: 'Fugitive Democracy' in: Seyla Benhabib (ed.): *Democracy and Difference* (Princeton, NJ: Princeton University Press 1996), p. 43.
11. Seyla Benhabib: 'The Democratic Moment and the Problem of Difference' and 'Toward a Deliberative of Democratic Legitimacy' both in: ibid. pp. 3–18 and 67–94.
12. Benjamin Barber: 'Foundationalism and Democracy' in: ibid. pp. 348–59. Some of the ideas presented in the article stemmed from earlier deliberations. See particularly Barber's *Strong Democracy* (Berkeley/Los Angeles: University of California Press 1984), and his collection of essays *A Passion for Democracy* (Princeton, NJ: Princeton University Press 1998).

Chapter 7

Justice and Injustice

John Rawls' re-invention of political philosophy: *A Theory of Justice* ● Distributive justice and justice as fairness ● 'A community of justice': a community to form all other communities ● Robert Nozick's critique of Rawls' distributive liberalism ● Nozick's questioning of Rawls from an extreme libertarian point of view ● Robert Paul Wolff's secondment of Nozick from a Marxist perspective ● Michael Walzer's answer to Wolff's critique: insisting on the multiple spheres of justice ● The existence of non-transcendable boundaries ● Judith Shklar's simplification of Walzer's model: the distinction between political equality and social injustice ● Voting and earning ● The solution: the many dimensions of citizenship ● Ronald Dworkin's emphasis on rights in relation to questions of social and political dimensions of citizenship

The rise of capitalism and the development of social inequality appear to be symmetrical. Yet, as the Czech-British social theorist Ernest Gellner has reminded us, social inequality in modern industrialised societies is confined to a limited spectrum mainly because inequality no longer appears as naturalised and untranscendendable as it did during feudalist times. American society is no exception to the rule, but what distinguishes the United States from other capitalist societies is the peculiar relationship between political equality and social inequality. The hypothesis here is that because the Americans were the first to aim at political equality, America's concern with and interpretation of social inequality differs fundamentally from European and/or Europeanised societies. Such a different perspective finds its intellectual expression in the various American attempts to conceptualise justice. In an attempt to see how American thinkers have tried to conceptualise justice and injustice we will first look at John Rawls' groundbreaking study *A Theory of Justice* and the criticism it provoked. Second, we will look at alternative approaches to justice, to be found most prominently in Michael Walzer's reasoning on the different *Spheres of Justice*. In a third step we will take a closer look at conceptualisations of justice, which take the particular American experiences into account. It is the American insistence on the rhetoric of rights, as theorised in Ronald Dworkin's *Taking Rights Seriously* and Judith Shklar's *American Citizenship*, that provides us with insight into how America has attempted to come to terms with social inequality.

John Rawls' modern classic *A Theory of Justice* begins with the simple assumption that as human beings we all agree that there should be a sphere or realm in individuals' lives that in principle remains free of injustice.[1] This should be so even if an entire society were to benefit from an overall abstract notion of justice. Put differently, collective forms of justice find their limitations where individual liberty is concerned. Any modern understanding of justice must take this restriction into account. Yet it is exactly this relationship between individual rights and common notions of justice that, according to Rawls, needs a proper philosophical grounding. Rawls asks what it means when we mutually agree to acknowledge principles of justice that protect our individual liberties. Furthermore, he questions exactly how basic social institutions can be made to function according to such shared understanding.

Rawls is aware of the strong normative implications of such reasoning on justice and recognises that in a well-ordered society both the individual and the institutional dimension would function properly only in accordance with these preconditions. Yet Rawls also recognises that in the real world, societies debate and have disagreements about what is just and what isn't. What is needed then is a closer inspection of the relationship between the individual and the institutional dimension, in particular how a society regulates itself in terms of what it itself conceives to be 'just'.

Rawls locates his own efforts in the liberal philosophical tradition of social contract theories and he thus refers directly to the reasoning of Locke, Rousseau and Kant. Yet Rawls differs from his predecessors in that he aims at a higher form of synthesis: no longer must we imagine a social contract as if we were in a position to introduce a completely new social and political system. In contrast, Rawls' notion of the social contract refers to original motifs, norms and values of justice that citizens, if asked hypothetically, would agree upon, as it were in their own interest to do so. All further conceptualisations and arrangements would be based on this affirmation of a principle of justice – a principle that he describes as 'justice as fairness'. In Rawls' further conceptualisation of justice as fairness, the original position of equality takes on the same theoretical role that the 'state of nature' played in the older social contract theory. With his conceptualisation of the original position and of justice as fairness, Rawls also rejects the utilitarian models of justice; there is, for example, no reasoning of the principle of 'the greatest happiness for the greatest number of people'. Furthermore Rawls emphasises the notion of 'being reasonable' against a perception of mankind that sees individuals solely as human beings who are pursuing their own interests. To be more precise, it is Rawls' conviction that the utilitarian conceptions suffer from a serious weakness in that they have no appropriate notion or definition of what 'good' means and they cannot explain how exactly the good could be distributed in a fair way. Once models which are based on charging something against something else (in this case giving up private advantages or interests for a common good from which everyone would benefit) are excluded, other questions arise: what exactly is it that grounds and guides our principles of decision-making? And why should we accept the principle of justice in the first instance?

According to Rawls, the answers to these questions are to be found in a combined view that stresses justice as fairness and allows the good to be seen as something that may be reasonably achieved. How would such a combination be possible? The answer is simple – through the idea of the social community. According to Rawls, human beings become stronger and achieve more by means of association; for Rawls there is, for example, a mutual beneficial dimension to the formation of social groups. Once the different capacities of individuals leave the purely private realm and enter the social sphere of the community, everybody's life will be enriched. In other words, if individuals agree on minimal principles of fairness, every individual would benefit from it. This form of reasoning somehow resembles utilitarian thinking, yet it should not be mistaken as such. In opposition to such reasoning stands the idea of a well-ordered social community as a community which forms the basis for all other forms of communities.

Rawls uses the analogy of a game that is played with different players and different roles to counter views that see disintegrating mechanisms as being stronger: a game with fair rules is played by opposing players with the objective of a good game; there is thus no absolute division of labour. Similarly, individuals in a well-ordered society feel obliged to follow societal rules in order to achieve a just society. Here, Rawls reminds us again of how important it is to respect individual liberty. It is only through not destroying the other player that we can continue to play the game. Only respecting the liberty of other individuals – fair play in other words – enables us to achieve justice. Yet in order to play a game called 'society', it is necessary that all players have roughly equal means before entering the 'game'– a precondition that justifies the labelling of Rawls' approach as a model of 'distributive justice'.

Rawls' conceptualisation of political philosophy in the form of distributive justice did not remain without its critics. Robert Nozick, a close colleague from Harvard, directly challenged Rawls' views. His *Anarchy, State, and Utopia* must be read as a direct counterproposal to Rawls conception of distributive justice.[2] Writing from a radical libertarian point of view, Nozick takes issue with all conceptualisations that go beyond the minimal state. His main objection to models that go further than the minimal state, which warrants that no bodily harm is being done and no physical threat is carried out, is that the pattern of principles which would guide the model of distributive justice remains unspecific, if not obscure. Rawls' model does not provide answers to such questions as: who would be entitled to be on the receiving end of the distribution? Who distributes? And what exactly are the goods that are going to be distributed? Further-more, what sort of rights and entitlements are we looking at and what sort of rights and entitlements will be preferred in the model of distributive justice? Will they be only ends-oriented, as Rawls suggests? What about the means, don't they have to be just as well? To complicate matters even further: if it is true that there is also a historical dimension to Rawls's model, how can one distinguish between different legitimate claims of fair distribution? Will that depend on the individual points of entry into society? And finally, will people who are not in accordance with the principle of distributive justice be allowed to exit?

As with Nozick, the abstractness of Rawls' theory of distributive justice was a particular target for another critic, the radical philosopher Robert Paul Wolff. Wolff's profound critique of Rawls' theory of justice in *Understanding Rawls* vehemently took issue with the seemingly 'neutral' dimension of Rawls' work.[3] Yet Wolff's critique is that of a radical who rather sym-pathises with Rawls and who is opposed to the other extreme of Nozick's libertarian liberalism. Wolff criticises the lack of concrete facts on the different social realities in the social, economic and political realms with the aim of showing that Rawls doesn't go far enough. Furthermore, Wolff maintains that Rawls' abstract theory masks nothing but a shameful reality; Wolff places *A Theory of Justice* historically among nineteenth-century attempts at an apology 'for an egalitarian brand of liberal welfare-state capitalism'.[4] In other words, it serves as an ideology.

Although Wolff further dismisses *A Theory of Justice* as being over-protective through its abstraction, he does concede that it serves some purpose to consider the notion of justice in more universal terms rather than deriving a notion of justice purely from small-scale social practices. Having declared his general openness to a more general theory of justice, Wolff then goes a step further in questioning *A Theory of Justice* by suggesting that one should consider the idea of gross inequality in terms of income, and the very fact that such inequality is derived from and is generated by existing economic forces, that is surplus production (the surplus being appropriated by those who own the means of production). According to *A Theory of Justice*, the inequality gap in income would be bridged through distribution, that is inequality surplus would be redistributed through the state while the economic principle would remain untouched. Wolff rejects such a model outright. For him, Rawls has no imagination and no proper understanding of the links that exist between politics and economics, hence his naivety about the neutral distributive state. In essence, Wolff's critique reveals that Rawls does not provide any account of the proper mechanisms and means of redistribution, and quite clearly there is no conceptualisation of the way political power works. In his critique, Wolff has already taken into account Rawls' fundamental assumption of a well-ordered society, that is the will of the citizens to accept and to submit to the rules of the distributive game. Yet, as Wolff has demonstrated, this formal model is flawed through the weak links that exist between politics (the state) and economics (a specific regime of production). Therefore what remains is a model that neglects specifics and is, in the words of Wolff, a model 'from which all significant historical, political, and social features have been removed'.[5] In this respect Rawls' theory resembles earlier models of classical political economy in which production remains untouched and inequality is dealt with in terms of social democratic conceptions of justice.

Wolff's critique, however, can itself be criticised in that it reduces everything to the Marxist line of production and surplus extraction that is to the economic sphere from which everything else stems. Thus Wolff himself neglects complicated mechanisms and the existence of different spheres, be they 'political', 'social' or 'cultural'. It is only through another critic, Michael Walzer, a social philosopher at Princeton University, that we begin to gain a more balanced viewpoint of the many links, realms and rich layers of justice that work to create a differentiated society.

The title of Walzer's study, *Spheres of Justice*, immediately indicates a different approach to the all-encompassing general view of Rawls.[6] Walzer suggests that there is not simply one notion of justice or one sphere of justice, but rather that an understanding of justice in modern society must be based on an acknowledgement of complex spheres of inequality (and in response an equally complex model of equality and justice). Walzer manages to clarify that there is a direct link between equality and 'abolitionist politics' that is the objective is to abolish the differences that are seen to be at the root of inequality and injustice. Yet, as the author warns us, this does not give us free rein to abolish all differences at all times; it might not even mean abolishing the major differences at any specific point in time. In order to tackle the problem properly, one must seek the root of the question, which is firmly grounded in the art of making distinctions and the art of differentiation. For Walzer, 'equality is simply the outcome of (this) art'[7] and it is precisely this art of differentiation (and the possibilities that arise from such an interpretation) that Walzer pinpoints as lacking in John Rawls' conceptualisation of justice.

In *Spheres of Justice* Walzer argues that there is not, and there probably never will be, a 'universal medium of exchange'. There is in other words not a central vantage point from which to tackle injustice and inequality in the general sense of the words: 'To search for unity is to misunderstand the subject matter of distributive justice'.[8] Walzer still favours a coherent approach but insists that it must start with the acceptance of pluralist forms of life and justice. Only if the analyst acknowledges a reality that is complex, and the analysis is truly pluralist in description, will there be a chance for a coherent pluralist answer to the challenges that multiple forms of injustice pose.

Walzer's preoccupation with the state may be explained by the fact that it is generally acknowledged as being the central agency in terms of distributive justice. Walzer demands that we learn from the experiences of the past: for example, in his view 'actually existing communism' has shown that a state which acts as an agent on behalf of simple and one-dimensional economic equality necessarily becomes oppressive, and if the state does not take precautionary measures through powerful control, monopolies and other competing forms of control would prevail.[9] The problem with this view is that in the end the state itself becomes the object of a fierce struggle. Modern democracies have become aware of this, as can be seen through their attempt to 'pluralise' power by instigating mechanisms of separation and checks and balances.

Walzer's major concern remains with the dilemma that once the political monopoly has fallen and once one has accepted the democratic rules in society and politics, there is no turning back to the model of simple, one-dimensional equality. To be sure, this could turn out to be problematic as, in order to positively spell out how complex equality works, one has, as Walzer stresses, 'to map out the entire social world'.[10] A major task indeed, and this is perhaps why Walzer himself sticks to a phenomenology that simply describes the boundaries between the different realms of life and also stresses that to respect these boundaries makes sense in a highly differentiated society.

Not by chance does Walzer introduce his phenomenology with a description and defence of the political community; it is after all the crucial community in which meaning is shared, certainly more so than in the other 'social' realms. The political community is also special in that it distributes itself as a commodity, that is membership cannot be distributed by some external mechanism, but only through its own members. It is also important to acknowledge the existence of various political communities and boundaries – assuming that even in the long run the world will not form one political community, governed by a proper, functioning global government. Once one has accepted the existence of different political communities and boundaries, the question of membership arises, that is if the entire world was just and free, the question of membership would never arise. Walzer argues realistically in this respect; no such global, free and just society is in sight – hence membership of one of the many political communities becomes crucial. Some communities are better than others – just as there are individuals who are better citizens than others. It is here that the peculiar American dimension of the argument becomes clear – after all it is the US that is the only country that in essence has had, and still has, an open debate on who should be admitted to its political community and who should not. Furthermore, it is the US that also had the most inclusive policies regarding the admission of strangers and the naturalisation of refugees and other immigrants. This clearly stands in contrast to other countries which – although formally acknowledged as being democratic – still have tyrannical traits in that they exclude people who share the same political territory, usually through withholding full political membership rights.

Having highlighted the peculiarities of the political realm and the essential need for political membership, the issue of the differentiated social bases of community membership still needs to be addressed. Whereas the political dimension has been acknowledged as being special in terms of distributive justice, the social realms differ. In discussing security, welfare, money and commodities, holding office, work, education, kinship, family and other love relationships, religious matters, recognition (that is status and prestige), democracy and power in institutional settings and, finally, rights, Walzer is keen to emphasise the existence of boundaries and the incompatibility of the respective realms.

The reason for treating these social realms as internally differentiated and as altogether different from the political realm simply refers to the fact that political means and ends can be and actually very often are in conflict with 'social' means and ends. Walzer uses the example of votes and economic success: votes do not directly translate into economic profit, while economic gain does not directly translate into political achievement. Once one loses sight of the distinctions between the political and the social realm and the differentiation process within the various social realms, the danger of totalitarianism begins to loom large. The acknowledgement of complex equality is therefore the safest insurance policy against totalitarian forms of control of differentiated societies.

Michael Walzer has given us a pluralist account of how to challenge injustice, yet he seems to have replaced the approach of Rawls with a pluralist approach that is so fuzzy in its contours that it becomes almost impossible to apply it to such a differentiated and complex society as the United States. The picture only becomes clearer if one reduces the complexity of justice and injustice to more concrete conceptual notions such as citizenship and rights. Pursuing this path is a scholar whose contributions have already been discussed, Judith N. Shklar, and a British–American scholar who has contributed considerably to American legal debates, Ronald Dworkin.

Judith Shklar's book *Faces of Injustice* must be read as a phenomenology of the general human conditions of injustice.[11] The crucial distinction in her book is the one between political injustice and individual misfortune. While political injustice is produced by and through the actions of other human beings, individual misfortune usually has almost 'natural' connotations, that is it is usually considered to be beyond human control and responsibility.[12]

In order to come to terms with the various forms of political injustice, the rhetoric of fairness was 'invented'. Shklar calls such a conception 'distributive' or 'primary' justice, referring to a system of institutions that prevent injustice through political means. In modern democracies in particular efforts are continuously made to 'channel' injustice in the sense that, although total justice will never be achieved and is probably something that people should not strive for, at least arbitrariness and cruelty are avoided and a fair process guaranteed. One of the measures that a democracy can take is to aim at maximum public participation in the decision-making process. Another measure would be to listen to protest and to open up channels to guarantee that voices of dissent can be heard.

Shklar acknowledges the fact that America never opted for models of overall justice and overall equality. Aware of the shortcomings of the European model of equality, America opted for a modified version that is equality of opportunity where political citizenship would guarantee equality and fairness while it would be up to the individuals to use this political equality to avoid the pitfalls of 'social' inequality. However, even this model has its shortcomings since it only reduces the extremes of inequality as far as is politically possible; it does not fully abolish them. In this respect Shklar criticises the limited attention span of primary justice. However, Shklar does not fully develop another model that would emphatically embrace the idea of 'secondary justice'. She only describes the contours of such a model.

In a compendium study, entitled *American Citizenship – The Quest for Inclusion*, Shklar elaborates on the earlier study and explores how the concepts of political and social rights are directly related to questions on injustice.[13] It is in this study that Shklar develops a broader notion of what 'secondary justice' could mean. Shklar is fully aware that the question of political membership is of primary importance as it sets the framework for all other aspects. She also shows that to insist only on formal membership and citizenship is to neglect the rich connotations of citizenship. Only when the social dimensions of citizenship are taken into account, and only when the relationship between 'the social' and 'the political' becomes clearer, will we reach a view that will allow us to explore the various aspects of justice in a comprehensive way.

On the question of political equality and citizenship Shklar acknowledges that there has always been a tension between an American ideology of citizenship which guarantees equality and an attempt to keep out unwelcome elements either through exclusion (by restricting immigration) or by limiting the voting rights of members of the political community. It is exactly this tension between a strong normative emphasis on the universal rights of citizens and the more particularistic practice when it came to reality that sets the American experience apart from others. 'We the people' sounded all-embracing but in practice could lead to exclusive practices. Shklar reminds us in particular of the exclusion of African Americans and women from full citizenship. Nevertheless, Shklar also stresses that the same excluded citizens had used and are still using exactly the normative ideas of the Constitution and the Bill of Rights to fight exclusion.

Social 'earning', however, is a more complicated social activity than political 'voting'. Usually each individual participates and is engaged in the two spheres – yet 'the political' is still being seen in terms of equality, whereas 'the social' is linked to notions of inequality and injustice. However, 'earning', economic independence and being a 'self-made' person has always been regarded as an activity which contributed considerably to the making of 'full' American citizenship. This is particularly true when one looks at the early period of American history: the founding of the republic could only take place because men were free of feudal bonds, that is, worked independently, until at a later stage the reverse became true. Shklar stresses here that the issue is self-respect and autonomy in terms of being an independent citizen who does not depend on other citizens. Seen in this light, the right to earn is not a human right but a 'local' condition contributing to 'full' citizenship. It is so important that anybody deprived of employment should be compensated for it, at least according to Shklar.

Shklar has explored the relationship between one important social realm and the political dimension of citizenship. It is not by chance that her study ends with a discussion of rights and the further distinction between social and political rights. Shklar emphasises that political rights must have primacy over social rights – but that does not necessarily mean that the social world is less important. As Shklar suggests, there is a strong relationship between the two and, as American history demonstrates, citizenship would be empty if deprived of these concrete social connotations. As a matter of fact, political rights can help to improve one's social status; they have inclusive dimensions, which could reach far beyond the purely 'political'. This is particularly true in the American context: here 'the political' always served to improve 'the social'.

The fact that rights can take on such a comprehensive meaning in America has been observed and studied by the legal scholar Ronald Dworkin, particularly in his study *Taking Rights Seriously*.[14] The general attempt of Dworkin is to conceptualise rights in such a way that, first, the political framework remains one of liberty and, second, that one can still remain sensible about the issue of equality/inequality. In his view the arrangements must be such that there is a balance between the common good and well-being and individual rights, that is constitutional politics must opt for the thin line between equality and freedom. The immediate questions that then arise are of course 'which equality?' and 'which freedom?' Dworkin distinguishes between two answers to this question. Citizens who uphold a liberal conception of justice must decide between an interpretation which favours the right to receive equal treatment, and an interpretation which favours the right to be treated equally. The first alternative demands that everyone receives the same goods or chances; the second alternative does not refer to the direct distribution of goods and chances but rather to equal treatment in the decision-making process which decides how goods and chances are distributed. The idea is not to inflate the first notion of absolute equal treatment because it could have a serious impact and devastating effect on the second notion in that the equilibrium between social rights and individual freedom could be destroyed – with the result that social rights would outflank individual liberty.

To be sure, Dworkin argues for a differentiated utilitarian model in which a liberal conception of justice provides the goods that are necessary to make a modern democracy function but that also dispensed with the all-embracing Rawlsian model of justice. The case that Dworkin argues is that an intrinsic connection between political and social rights exists. It is rights 'taken seriously' which have replaced the battle between the previously prominent views of the extremist alternative of 'liberty versus equality' and the related, somehow 'absolutist', models of justice. Avoiding the European trap of demanding absolute equality, it was indeed the United States that became the first country to experiment with a different understanding of rights, exploring the new dimensions of justice under a liberal spell.

Notes

1. John Rawls: *A Theory of Justice* (Cambridge, MA: Harvard University Press 1971).
2. Robert Nozick: *Anarchy, State, and Utopia* (Oxford: Blackwell 1975).
3. Robert Paul Wolff: *Understanding Rawls* (Princeton, NJ: Princeton University Press 1977).
4. Ibid. p. 195.
5. Ibid. p. 205.
6. Michael Walzer: *Spheres of Justice* (New York: Basic Books 1983).
7. Ibid. p. xv.
8. Ibid. p. 4.
9. Walzer assumes that the communist model of controlling the means of production more collectively can still be explained in terms of distributive justice. Opposed to Wolff's critique, which stressed the difference between distribution and production, Walzer's account is concerned with distribution.
10. *Spheres of Justice* p. 26.
11. Judith Shklar: *Faces of Injustice* (New Haven/London: Yale University Press 1990).
12. Shklar is aware of the fact that misfortune can sometimes develop into injustice, for example, when precautionary measures against natural disasters are not taken and help is not properly organised etc.
13. Judith Shklar: *American Citizenship* (Cambridge, MA: Harvard University Press 1991).
14. Ronald Dworkin: *Taking Rights Seriously* (Cambridge, MA: Harvard University Press 1978).

Chapter 8

Pluralism and Multiculturalism

Civil rights legislation in the 1960s and its consequences ● Nathan Glazer's insistence on the 'voluntary character' of ethnicity in America ● The result of social differentiation: we are all multiculturalists now ● New debates on pluralism and multiculturalism ● Charles Taylor's Canadian exploration of the problem of recognition ● *E pluribus unum:* Michael Walzer's response to Taylor ● Back to the problem of identity and difference: Anthony Appiah's phenomenology and conceptual separation of analytic categories and normative values ● Richard Rorty's rejection of a simple acceptance of multiculturalism ● Rorty's change of perspective: from spectator and victim to competitive individualism and difference ● Jeffrey C. Alexander's challenge to Rorty: rethinking civil society and its uncivil dimensions

The sociologist Nathan Glazer deserves the credit for being the first person to bring the emergence of an American ethnic pattern to our attention and into the public debate.[1] Glazer states that with the passing of three decisive acts, the Civil Rights Act, the Voting Rights Act and the Immigration Act (all introduced within two years, 1964 and 1965), real progress was made. Glazer considers these acts to be a considerable achievement because they established that the American nation – after a long struggle for civil rights – had officially agreed that the acceptance of divisive patterns along lines of ethnic background or definitions of race would no longer be tolerated.

Yet this is exactly where the more complicated story begins. Glazer sees it as a result of a somewhat cunning course of history that this introduction of civil rights legislation in effect had unforeseen consequences, in that it enforced a renewed self-definition and perception of ethnic belonging – this time only in the name of equality of opportunity: 'paradoxically, we then began an extensive effort to record the race, color, and (some) national origins of just about every student and employee and recipient of government benefits or services in the nation; to require public and private employers to undertake action to benefit given groups . . . This monumental restructuring of public policy to take into account the race, color, and national origin of individuals, it is argued by Federal administrators and courts, is required to enforce the laws against discrimination on these very grounds'.[2] Glazer further stresses that people considered this at first to be 'a transitional period . . . to that condition called for in the Constitution and the laws, when no account at all is to be taken of race, color, or national origin', yet he also reports that in time 'others (began to) see it as a direct contradiction of the Constitution and the laws, and of the consensus that emerged after long struggle in the middle 1960s'.[3]

Glazer's own position can be described as a position in between the two extremes. He argues against a selective misreading of American history that assumes that America's history can only be understood as a deeply racist one. Countering such a position Glazer maintains that there is nothing inherently racist about America. As a matter of fact, the author points out that the idea of America is rather inclusive, and that it became even more inclusive throughout the course of history – with the 'finishing touch' being the above mentioned legislation. Glazer also recounts the numerous problems encountered along the way: slavery in the South, segregation, the racist immigration policies in the late nineteenth century; yet he also stresses that with the abolition of not only slavery, but of all other legislative barriers in the twentieth century, America became the only country where citizens who were regarded as equal in the political sphere could still maintain a 'voluntary character of ethnicity' in the social sphere. Thus it is up to individuals to decide which path they want to pursue in terms of creating their identity. Glazer reminds his readers that 'we have not set either course, neither the one of eliminating all signs of ethnic identity – through force or through the attractions of assimilation – nor the other of providing the facilities for the maintenance of ethnic identity'.[4]

Glazer is correct in his critical observation and comment concerning the post-civil-rights period. Yet he is not very precise in terms of conceptualising increasing differentiation and the social change that has occurred since the mid-1960s. In the past – particularly in the late 1950s and 1960s of this century – activists from diverse ethnic backgrounds fought together for the common goal of civil rights. At present, however, the situation is quite different in that particularistic trends have become more prominent – and this is not only due to the new legislation, as Glazer maintains. To be sure, in the past the discourse had always bounced back and forth between particularistic and universalistic means and ends.[5] At present the situation is considerably different – sociologically and politically: first, oppressed minorities – such as the black community – must be looked at from a different angle; African Americans are no longer the largest minority group in the US, but simply another minority among the many in a multicultural society; second, formerly disadvantaged ethnic communities in themselves have become differentiated: comparatively speaking, the spectrum of what individuals of these formerly oppressed ethnic minority backgrounds can do and achieve is now considerably broader than in the past, but further than that most ethnic minorities are internally more differentiated than ever before. Both factors, 'inward' and 'outward' differentiation, now lie at the very heart of the current debates on multicultural identity: Americans have to come to terms with their identity, or better still their non-identity, in a changing American environment. Having said that, one has to bear in mind that in a highly differentiated structure 'fine distinctions' (Pierre Bourdieu) can at once become major sources of conflict. In the face of both the 'inward' and 'outward' differentiation processes individuals are challenged – and suddenly, defending or claiming group rights becomes a 'necessity' for determining one's individual identity. In this respect Glazer is right: we are all multiculturalists now.[6]

The basic premise of the following argument is to look at attempts that have tried to conceptualise this complicated differentiation process. It can be clearly demonstrated that within American intellectual discourse there have been and still are voices that address the problem of identity/non-identity from a 'universalistic' standpoint – whilst at the same time not forgetting their 'particularistic' roots. Amongst these voices are such intellectuals and scholars as Charles Taylor and Michael Walzer, Anthony Appiah and Richard Rorty, and finally Jeffrey C. Alexander. While Walzer and Taylor stand, as we will see, for two different sides of the pluralists' perspective, Appiah and Rorty represent two points of view along the edges of the pluralist spectrum; finally, with Jeffrey C. Alexander's discussion of the various dimensions of multiculturalist and pluralist discourse, an umbrella approach is provided.

In his *Multiculturalism and 'The Politics of Recognition'* the Canadian philosopher Charles Taylor attempted to reflect on the link that exists between universal egalitarian structures in modern democracies and specific, particularistic cultural identities.[7] At the root of the problem lies the radical change from pre-modern to modern times. The road to modernity led to what Taylor calls 'a collapse of social hierarchies',[8] hierarchies which were based on honour. The end of inherited rights gave rise to the modern sense of dignity, a recognition that everybody can have expectations in modern democratic society. Further differentiation within these modern democracies led to a more individualised notion of dignity and recognition; nowadays individuals want to be acknowledged not just as abstract citizens but as authentic individuals with a specific background.

According to Taylor, the logic of the argument started out as a rejection of particularistic ideals identified with inherited titles and honours. This old system of honour was replaced by a striving for universal ideas and rights, which were then finally incorporated and written into the very idea of citizenship. In recent times a further differentiation process occurred, which led to the rhetoric of authenticity. Again particularistic ideals are emphasised, yet with the difference that this time they were based on the notion of universal citizenship. Taylor associates the names of Rousseau and Herder with the changes described above. While the former prepared the ground for achieving equality in the modern sense of the word, the latter stood for the acknowledgement of authenticity – the acknowledgement of real individual human character as something worth striving for. According to Taylor, two ideal-type models of modern liberal democracy exist, one that favours the 'politics of equal respect, as enshrined in a liberalism of rights' but is 'inhospitable to difference, because (a) it insists on uniform application of the rules defining these rights, without exception, and (b) it is suspicious of collective goals';[9] the other is a model that finds different answers to the problems of (a) and (b): This form would not 'call for the invariant defense of *certain* rights . . . There would be no question of cultural differences determining the application of *habeas corpus* for example. But they distinguish these fundamental rights from the broad range of immunities and presumptions of uniform treatment that have sprung up in modern cultures . . . they are willing to weigh the importance of cultural survival, and opt sometimes in favour of the latter'.[10] Taylor concludes that such a model would, in the last instance, not be grounded in procedures but in judgements about the good life. Seen in the light of an increasingly multicultural society, the purely procedural model does not seem to hold much of a future. Taylor therefore opts for the second model, where the 'demand for recognition is now explicit'. Yet Taylor has no illusions about the complicated mechanisms and does not anticipate a multicultural Utopia. He demands only that other cultures and individuals of other cultures be taken more seriously. Whether this will eventually lead to a 'fusion' remains to be seen. In Taylor's view we will first have to engage in a 'fusion of horizons' and to achieve an acceptance of authenticity before we can start thinking about the course liberal society might take.

One of the respondents to Taylor's essay was the American philosopher Michael Walzer. Overall he supports Taylor's proposal of the second model of liberalism, yet adds that within this option the problem of differences within the differing individuals needs to be taken more seriously. In respect of this problem he suggests the inclusion of some of the elements of the procedural model into the second model. To be sure, Walzer notes that such an option would be particularly viable for a country like the United States, which, after all, differs from Canada in many respects: there is no Quebec, that is a strong regional and linguistic stronghold. In a contribution to the *Harvard Encyclopaedia of American Ethnic Groups* Walzer has elaborated on what pluralism could mean in the context of a liberal society like the United States.[11] According to Walzer, pluralism in the strong sense of the word (one country, many peoples) had only been possible under non-democratic forms of government; Walzer refers to the empires of the past, the British Empire and also the Soviet Union. Only one exception to the rule exists, the United States – and this may be due to peculiar circumstances. In contrast to the Old World, the pluralism of the New World was one of the outcomes of being an immigrant society, not an empire – a first new nation where the different ethnic communities were never based in one specific territory. What distinguished the United States further was that politically the immigrants became citizens of the United States (the 'universal' dimension), yet in all other aspects, culturally, religiously and linguistically they maintained their specific backgrounds (the 'particularistic' dimension). The original idea had been that in the future these people of different origins would become one – as expressed in the slogan *E pluribus unum* (out of many – one). Yet the idea of the melting pot did not remain unchallenged and, indeed, as the practice showed, the motto of *E pluribus unum* could also be interpreted as 'Within one – many', and over the course of two centuries both sides have claimed that their interpretation is the 'correct' one. It is Walzer's hypothesis that finally a balance, if not a compromise, had been achieved. It is now possible to have both ethnic pluralism and a united republic. With regard to how this balance was achieved, Walzer stresses that when it comes to private matters, Americans are sociable, that is, they prefer to stay in their specific, often ethnic environment; yet when it comes to politics, Americans are deeply individualistic, that is, the government relies on the contributions of individuals – not representatives of certain groups. Of course it is also true that ethnic minorities try to influence politics, but Walzer relativises these efforts: to achieve something, a particular ethnic group will have to join a larger effort, it relies on coalitions and political alliances – otherwise it would never achieve anything. Thus no ethnic group can take absolute control of all political institutions.

What applies to politics also applies to a certain extent to the social world; American ethnic groups are usually not 'closed shops'; no-one is in a position to determine who will join and who should leave; they are dependent on voluntary contributions of individuals and on the will of individuals to join associations. Individual space and decision-making is at the heart of the American liberal model. This has positive as well as negative effects; 'positive' insofar as ethnic groups operating on a voluntary basis create an environment that is socially and perhaps politically relevant to the individuals involved; 'negative' insofar as there is a hard core of voluntary contributors who are more engaged than others – which often results in a situation where 'free-riders' profit from the actions of the core community, thus creating a certain imbalance within their own respective community. Yet these problems should not cloud our view of the fact that, as Walzer argues in another collection of essays, *What it means to be an American*, the United States is the only country where it has been possible and is still possible to have both assimilation and maintain one's difference.[12] To be sure, there are waves or cycles in American history. Sometimes the Americanness, that is, the option of assimilation appears to be stronger, while at other times the insistence on being different is more prevalent. However, individuals are free to choose which side of the hyphen they want to be, for example either *German*-American or German-*American*. Normatively speaking, it is not up to the central government to decide; practically speaking, Walzer knows that there have been times when there was high demand to opt in favour of Americanisation – politically and culturally. Those were the times when America appeared as less liberal and less pluralistic than it promised to be. Particularly when looking at how African Americans featured in these cycles, it becomes evident that American society has over decades of its history been negligent in striving to achieve public happiness for all.

In order to explore the darker sides of the options of 'hyphenated-nationalities' within liberal societies, it is useful to turn to the work of the social philosopher Anthony Appiah. In his *Color Conscience*, Appiah argues against all attempts at dividing the human race into different races and related cultures.[13] Rather he proposes the idea of differentiating between the analytical and the normative discourse of analysis. On the analytical level, Appiah suggests using a Sartrean approach: racism and its social consequences can indeed be phenomenologically observed; yet at the same time the observer must not confuse social cultural difference with biology (a view which usually stems from essentialising the social fact that individuals and groups are judged by other human beings and groups on the basis of the colour of their skin). For the analysis of historical discourses, Appiah's proposal would involve reflecting upon and investigating with a critical eye such labels as 'Africans', 'Negroes', 'Coloured People', 'Blacks', 'Afro-Americans' or 'African Americans'. It would not only mean writing the history of these signifiers, but also taking a closer look at their social and political implications and their possible effects.

Appiah warns against confusing the two levels of discourse: what seems to be acceptable on the analytical level is completely unacceptable on the normative level. He has no doubts that ethnic identity could become a forum for the purpose of confronting racism, yet he warns against making ethnic identity a new cause for future tyranny. Here, the social philosopher argues for making an intellectual effort: he aims at maintaining a balance between the meaning in difference of what he calls 'human identity' on one side, and the fundamental moral unity which is valid for humanity as a whole on the other side. Anthony Appiah has thus elevated the discourse of identity and difference to a new level – a new level where it is possible to discuss identity and/or even non-identity and how it relates to difference, without forgetting the pace-setting normative values.

Yet we should not forget that behind all intellectual statements lurk concrete social conditions, and behind all the talk about differences it is not difficult to identify larger drifts in and out of modern society. Multicultural America can serve as a good example. The change of macro-sociological patterns – for example demographic shifts resulting from changing immigration patterns – has had an impact on the micro-level – from shifting patterns of interaction to identity-formation processes of individuals. Thus when individual lifestyles become crucial, 'fine distinctions' can suddenly turn into major forces of identity formation processes. The re-emergence of the particularistic creed serves precisely the purpose of differentiating oneself from one's social group, and that which applies to daily life is necessarily repeated on the intellectual level as well. Thus much of the current rhetoric of multiple yet separate identities – most prominent in the field of 'cultural studies' – can be interpreted as a response to the differentiation process and internal stratification of modern society. Having said this, one must bear in mind that it is a false response; it simply reiterates and reinforces the 'Bennettonisation' (Henry Louis Gates) of society and culture on an intellectual level without breaking down the boundaries of biologically or culturally 'grounded' racist talk. According to Anthony Appiah it is the task of intellectuals to resist such 'imperialism of identity'. One must, however, question whether rounding off the sequence with the promotion of a new 'universal universalism' actually takes difference into account; does it make sense and does it really provide an answer to the salient questions as outlined above? In order to answer this question, one should take account of Richard Rorty's discussion on leftist thought in twentieth century America before finally delving into the notions of multiculturalism in American civil society as outlined by Jeffrey C. Alexander.

In *Achieving Our Country* Richard Rorty discusses the contemporary state of the American political left.[14] This discussion is directly relevant to our problem since Rorty takes on what he calls the 'Foucauldian' 'cultural Left'. According to the critic, the cultural Left is obsessed with 'otherness', 'ineradicable stigma' and the 'ubiqity of power' – hence it is only logical that 'Satan' and 'original sin' are the 'problems' the Foucauldian Left is preoccupied with. (Of course Rorty is speaking metaphorically: 'Satan' refers to the all-powerful social system, while 'original sin' refers to the fact that the social system seems to be so prevalent that to be part of it would mean exercising some of its structural power – regardless of individual positions or views.) The use of metaphysical metaphors suggests that Rorty regards the theoretical efforts from which the cultural Left derives its concepts as the secularised equivalent to religion. What Rorty wants to emphasise here is that there is nothing in the American leftist perception of Lacan's 'impossible objects of desire', Derrida's notion of 'differential subjectivity', or Foucault's notion of power which suggests that there could be such a thing as a political agent. (As a matter of fact, according to the criticised line of reasoning, it does not even make sense to talk about individuals and individuality any more.) As power becomes structural, it also becomes invisible – in short, metaphysical. Politically, Rorty considers this to be a disaster. If difference and otherness are preserved and perpetuated as counterweights to the structural powers that be, there can no longer be a sense of common ground – maybe apart from the sum of all differences. (It would indeed be deeply enshrined in the logic of the sum of all differences to be unable to pursue a common cause; not even laws could be proposed from such a standpoint – since it is the essence of law to abstract from all differences in order to make it applicable to all individuals.) It is such internal contradictions of 'the politics of difference' that lead Rorty to the verdict that if such a path were to be pursued further, deliberative leftist politics would cease to exist.

Rorty promotes a radical paradigm change: if there is to be a successful American Left in the future, it would have to see people no longer as mere spectators and victims, but rather as agents pursuing individual goals – and it would only be through individual achievement that difference would be respected and treated accordingly. But how can such a state of individual achievement and difference be reached? Rorty stresses that maintaining difference for its own sake makes little sense; logically then, for him the 'romance of endless diversity', not 'multiculturalism', is the solution. Multi-culturalism only 'suggests a morality of live-and-let-live, a politics of side-by-side development in which members of distinct cultures preserve and protect their own culture against the incursions of others, cultures'.[15] In opposition to such a viewpoint, Rorty suggests pursuing the Hegelian project of the struggle for acceptance, that is, competition, arguments and discussion between members of various cultures, in order to achieve a synthesis, a new and better culture, consisting of a 'variety in unity'. Furthermore, Rorty remarks that the solution can only be a political one – based on shared and reliable democratic institutions and citizenship.[16]

However, in Rorty's account, the social realm remains somehow void. He might be a good philosopher and a decent political theorist, yet he has little to say about the social and societal conditions under which individualism and difference thus conceived could compete and indeed flourish. There is, for example, nothing in Rorty's account that explains why it is that we are now witnessing the numerous discussions about the possible contradictions between political and social, individual and group rights. Rorty can certainly provide answers when it comes to the normative implications, but he is at odds when discussing the real social dimensions of individual competition and difference. In particular he seems to have absolutely no clear notion of how differentiated and complex modern society can be; furthermore, he has no notion of any of the universalistic dimensions that lie behind citizenship.

In response to Rorty's intellectual void, the conceptual framework of Jeffrey C. Alexander – particularly his conceptualisation of modern, differentiated civil society – affords us an understanding of the complicated sociological side of the argument on difference. In order to acknowledge the depth of Alexander's point of view, we must take a brief look at intellectual history: Alexander distinguishes between three different forms of civil society. 'Civil society 1' was first conceptualised by such thinkers as Ferguson and Smith, Rousseau, Hegel and Tocqueville, and referred to an early umbrella-like variety of institutions outside the state: that is, religious groups, private and public organisations, public opinion and institutions. In contrast, 'civil society 2' stands not for a further elaboration of the idea, as one would expect, but rather for a narrowed-down version of the original concept in that civil society becomes associated solely with market capitalism. Political equality and rights, in short, citizenship, are denounced as being only formally equal. Instead of political equality, Marx in particular preferred to promote substantive social equality. It is indeed a cunning move within history that it proved to be the Right that interpreted and perpetuated this logic in that they attempted to abolish all social controls in order to give more space to the market. The Left was no better in that they thought it appropriate to abolish the market altogether – either practically as is witnessed in the communist countries or theoretically as displayed in much of Western Marxist thought. Yet, as we approach the end of the century, we are witness to the emergence of 'civil society 3' – a society in which differentiation leads to a social realm that can be explained neither by referring to the state nor the capitalist market alone. Alexander describes this social realm as 'a solidary sphere in which a certain kind of universalising community comes gradually to be defined and to some degree enforced.'[17] He further explains: 'To the degree this solidary community exists, it is exhibited by 'public opinion', possesses its own cultural codes and narratives in a democratic idiom, is patterned by a set of peculiar institutions, most notably legal and journalistic ones, and is visible in historically distinctive sets of international practices like civility, equality, criticism, and respect.' He adds finally: 'This kind of civil community can never exist as such; it can only "to one degree or another". One reason is that it is always interconnected with, and interpenetrated by, other more and less differentiated spheres which have their own criteria of justice and their own system of rewards. There is no reason to privilege any one of these non-civil spheres over any other.'

These quotes can be read as an abstract of Alexander's attempts at conceptualising differentiation within modern society. In particular, the development of different social spheres, each with its own relative autonomy that is irreducible to other spheres, and also the communication between the different spheres seem to be central to an understanding of how modern civil society functions. It also becomes clear that to select one discourse above another means to not only conceptualise late twentieth-century civil society in terms of nineteenth-century developments, but more crucially, it also means giving in to the uncivil dimensions of civil society. Whether socialists want to get rid of civil society, because it is utterly bourgeois, or whether radical feminists argue that civil society is inherently patriarchical, or whether black nationalists think of racism as a natural part of civil society – all these discourses suffer from the generalisation of particular discourses and deny the complexity of modern civil society. Furthermore, as Alexander notes, these highly selective uncivil discourses are deeply anti-individualist in that they reject the unique history of individualism in Western societies – particularly the contributions of Christianity, the Renaissance, the Reformation, the Enlightenment and Romanticism to modern civil society.

To sum up, what Alexander's conception of civil society allows us to do is not only to be critical of the anti-individualist discourse of the Foucauldian Left; its further advantage is that it also allows us to conceptualise the sometimes uncivil multicultural discourses of civil society.

Alexander's conclusion serves as a reminder of an observation made by the black scholar C.L.R. James. Asked to comment on the new development of 'black studies' he said (and his comment can also be regarded as being relevant to any other particularistic field of study, or any dogmatic insistence on difference, be it cultural, or on religious grounds): 'to talk to me about black studies as if it's something that concerned black people is an utter denial. This is the history of Western Civilisation. I can't see it otherwise. This is the history that black people and white people and all serious students of modern history and the history of the world have to know. To say it's some kind of ethnic problem is a lot of nonsense.'[18]

Notes

1. In numerous books – some more theoretically grounded, others more empirically oriented – Glazer has tried to clarify the complex composition of the American people and the related political tensions stemming from it, see for example Glazer's *Beyond the Melting Pot* (together with Patrick Monyhan; Cambridge, MA: MIT Press 1970) and the collection *Ethnic Dilemmas, 1964-1982*, (Cambridge, MA: Harvard University Press 1983). For what follows, see particularly his study *Affirmative Discrimination: Ethnic Inequality and Public Policy* (New York: Basic Books 1975). An excerpt was reprinted in Ronald Takaki (ed.): *From Different Shores* (New York/Oxford: Oxford University Press 1994), pp. 11–23.

2. *Affirmative Discrimination*, exerpt as published in *From Different Shores*, p. 11.

3. Ibid. p. 11.

4. Ibid. p. 22.

5. This is particularly true for the Afro-American community. The debates between W.E.B. Du Bois and Booker T. Washington and Martin Luther King and Malcolm X are legendary in this respect.

6. Nathan Glazer: *We Are All Multiculturalists Now* (Cambridge, MA: Harvard University Press 1997).

7. Charles Taylor: *Multiculturalism and 'The Politics of Recognition'* (Princeton, NJ: Princeton University Press 1992).

8. Ibid. p. 26.

9. Ibid. p. 60.

10. Ibid. p. 61.

11. Michael Walzer: 'Pluralism – A Political Perspective' in: Stephan Thernstrom: *Harvard Encyclopedia of American Ethnic Groups* (Cambridge, MA: The Belknap Press of Harvard University Press 1980), pp. 781–7.

12. Michael Walzer: *What it means to be an American* (New York: Marsilio 1992).

13. K. Anthony Appiah and Amy Gutmann: *Color Conscious* (Princeton, NJ: Princeton University Press 1996).

14. Richard Rorty: *Achieving Our Country – Leftist Thought in Twentieth-Century America* (Cambridge, MA 1998). The title 'Achieving Our Country' is taken from James Baldwin's essay 'The Fire Next Time': 'If we – and now I mean the relatively conscious whites and the relatively conscious blacks, who must, like lovers, insist on, or create, the consciousness of the others – do not falter in our

duty now, we may be able, handful that we are, to end the racial nightmare, and achieve our country, and change the world.' (Baldwin as quoted by Rorty, p. 12f).

15. Ibid. p. 24.
16. This seems to be the major contradiction in Rorty: he supports the idea of citizenship, yet he abhors everything that reminds him of universalism or universal values.
17. 'Civil Society I, II, III' in: Jeffrey C. Alexander: *Real Civil Societies* (London: SAGE 1998), pp. 1–19. This quote and the next two can be found on p. 7.
18. C.L.R. James (ed. Anna Grimshaw): *The C.L.R. James Reader* (New York/ Oxford: Blackwell 1992), p. 397.

Chapter 9

Civil Society, Social Theory and the Task of Intellectuals

Richard Flacks' account of democratic history-making ● 1989 and the 'roll-on' effects on American social theory ● The rediscovery of the concept of civil society and its applications: Jean L. Cohen and Andrew Arato ● The radicalisation of the civil society debate: Jeffrey C. Isaac's critique of 'The Strange Silence of Political Theory' and Jeffrey C. Goldfarb's concretisation of Isaac's critique ● Rethinking the role of intellectuals in modern American civil society ● The feminist conceptualisation of the public and the private sphere ● The distinction between republican and liberal voices in feminist discourse ● Mary P. Ryan's counternarrative and the feminisation of the American Jeremiad

Richard Flacks, one of the prominent activists of the American 1960s student movement and a disciple of Mills, reviewed what had happened since Thorstein Veblen and C. Wright Mills had delivered their pragmatism–inspired political and sociological sermons. Flacks' study, entitled *Making History – The American Left and the American Mind*, must be interpreted as an attempt to reconsider and to bring up to date the project of 'participatory democracy' and the role the left and its intellectuals played within it.[1] Flacks' account was another attempt to close the gap that Veblen and Mills had discovered earlier on – the gap between an undemocratic and unchecked institutional power elite making history and a mass of powerless individuals striving for more democratic means to make history.[2] In Flacks' account, the Left's and the liberals' attempt to understand democracy aimed at 'cutting back' on structural dimensions of power and revitalising democracy for the individuals. This, as Flacks states, was easier said than done – particularly in a country where the relationship between democracy and individualism was very strong. As Flacks rightly observes, this tradition leads to the inclination to interpret the world in terms of individual action and the organisation of daily life rather than in terms of social relationships and larger influential structures. Since the relationship between democracy and individualism is so fundamental to the American creed, citizens tend to view politics as somewhat instrumental: politics is used in terms of means – not of ends. Flacks acknowledges that with very few exceptions the American Leftist intellectual had failed to see this: 'The seductive power of the consumer package lies in the fact that house, car and related equipment are both symbolic and real means to realise the cultural promise of personal freedom, interdependence, privacy, and choice'.[3] But what the liberal Left also failed to conceptualise was that 'standardised consumption provides only limited material for the formation and maintenance of identity and only momentary escape from inevitable troubles, pain and grief'.[4] Flacks here hints at a serious lack of communication: where ordinary Americans were making life, not history, the dogmatic left and its intellectuals demanded that history be made. What both sides failed to see was the connection that existed between the two.

However, Flacks notes that in the past there have been moments where the American left and its intellectual representatives were strong and could relate to America as a whole, especially when they reflected upon the relationship that exists so far as one has to 'make history' in order to 'make life'. Yet in order to prolong these rare moments the Left would have needed a deeper understanding of exceptionalist conditions in America. By referring to exceptionalist circumstances Flacks hints at the peculiar American social history with its fragmented characters, split communities and separated publics.

For Flacks there is a further lesson to be learned: if the liberal Left really wants to succeed, it has to be oriented towards universal values. It must aim at general transformation – not only defend or fight for the emancipation of particular communities or pursuing and securing particular rights. Yet it would be wrong to throw the baby out with the bathwater. The existence of diverse communities and publics means also that no central committee exists, no major left party, no national organisation. However, what does exist within the Left is an infrastructure, a potential for publics – publics that are devoted to the further democratisation of history – making. Flacks never tires of stressing that this heterogeneous public infrastructure could prove crucial in revitalising American civil society – a project that had been paramount for intellectuals, from Ralph Waldo Emerson and John Dewey to Thorstein Veblen and C. Wright Mills.

In the end Flacks acknowledges that there is still a long way to go: culturally America is certainly pluralistic – probably more so than ever before; yet, America is also class-dominated and elitist in its decision-making processes. One way of closing this gap would be the pursuit of a clear agenda, a public philosophy that would enable one to measure the success (or failure) of democratic history-making. Promoting this notion should be the task of the intellectuals. Flacks is aware of the dilemma within this proposal: again it would be an elite that would be the 'intellectual spearhead' – yet for the first time it would be an elite well aware of its own future demise in a fully democratised civil society. To pursue this task, the left would have to democratise itself – both practically and conceptually. According to Flacks this has not yet been achieved. In his concluding remarks he writes: 'What is wrong, from my point of view, is that people lack the historical awareness and the language to articulate a generalised vision of democracy'.[5]

What distinguishes Richard Flacks' account of the liberal Left from other critiques, such as those of the neo-liberals and neo-conservatives, is its insistence on the American promise of freedom and equality without diminishing the importance of one for the sake of the other. It is precisely this insistence on balance which other critics failed to recognise. In this respect the tone of criticism of former radicals, now turned neo-liberals and neo-conservatives, like Norman Podhoretz, David Horowitz, or Daniel Bell (to name the most prominent critics), remained, in a way, anti-Jeremiadan, even anti-American.[6] Although their critiques should not be entirely rejected – as a shot of realism is always helpful – their hyper-realism and defence of the status quo failed precisely because they insisted on the 'must have' of an elite and Capitalism (with capital 'C'). What these critics seemed not to realise was that their insistence on the possibility of exchanges that should normally be blocked (just as Michael Walzer has pointed out) in effect served to provoke a deeply held American sentiment, namely the insistence on an intellectual, non-hereditary elite in which the better argument could prevail – not solely the money that had been inherited. Both the Founding Fathers of the American republic and the cementation through the Jacksonian Age are examples of this. The neo-liberals and neo-conservatives lost sight of the fact that it was both the democratisation and equality aspects of property that had made America great, and this is precisely what Flacks' liberal Left critique hints at. It is therefore hardly surprising that by the end of the 1980s, and after a short and fashionable boom, neo-liberal and neo-conservative ideas had indeed become a part of history. By American standards and in the course of almost 250 years, the short affair with these ideas seems to have been little more than an aberration. Yet history sometimes holds surprising twists: by 1989 the American Left was in an equal state of turmoil due to the events that are associated with these chiffres and the impact they had on the political agenda of pursuing the cause of social justice.

There is no better source for documentation on the impact that international events and developments had on the renewal of American intellectual debates than in Jean L. Cohen and Andrew Arato's groundbreaking study *Civil Society and Political Theory*. It documented that it is simply not correct to view American debates as isolated from international discussions or following a somehow exceptionalist intellectual path.[7] As the authors made clear from the outset, their enterprise must be seen in the context of the international debates that began in the late 1970s and lasted throughout the 1980s – in particular the Anti-Totalitarianism debates in France, the discussion in former West–Germany on statism (not least as represented by the Social Democratic Party and – in reaction to the SPD in power – the new social movements). Furthermore, the transition from military dictatorship to democracy in many South American countries and finally the renewal of the social contract in Eastern Europe must be taken into consideration. Conceptually it was the Polish debates in particular, centred around the self-limiting character of the concept of civil society – seen as being both the agent and result of the social transformation observed – that helped Cohen and Arato to formulate their own epistemological focus. Their comprehensive study aims both at a defence and a further democratisation of civil society in a time where new forms of self-organisation and self-constitution became apparent and stood to challenge older notions of civil society. In their discussion of the various other attempts at conceptualising modern society, Cohen and Arato criticise the reliance on older dichotomous models that clearly separated the state from society. This, according to the authors, is very much an undifferentiated nineteenth-century view. In their own conceptualisation of modern civil society, Cohen and Arato preferred to build on a distinction which had first been introduced by the German social philosopher Jürgen Habermas. According to his theory, modern civil society has become so differentiated that it makes more sense to replace the old state–society distinction with two new concepts that allow one to grasp the complicated differentiation processes that underpin modern society, that is, the system and the lifeworld. While the former is based on instrumental action and leads to the creation of the state with its political subsystems in conjunction with the development of the modern economic system, the latter stands for non-instrumental, communicative action which is 'at work' in the cultural realm. As Cohen and Arato stress, Habermas is not so naïve as to suggest that everything in the modern world is actually wonderful when it is seen as being differentiated and seen through the lens of system and lifeworld. Quite the contrary, a complex relationship between the two realms exists; most of the conflicts within modern society result from a colonisation process whereby the system relies on the lifeworld resources of communicative action in order to make it function. As a consequence the system begins to dominate and finally to colonise the lifeworld. It is at this point that Cohen and Arato introduce another notion, namely that this colonisation process also meets resistance; through people's demands and struggles, institutional barriers such as political and social rights were introduced – with the effect of preventing total domination. In this context the creation and development of a public sphere in which public reasoning and deliberation could emerge and conflicts be peacefully resolved also played an important role. In order to facilitate this development, the further differentiation between a public and a private sphere was crucial. This distinction served as a barrier that the state had to respect: within the legal framework privacy became a protected realm. Preserving these boundaries between system and lifeworld is part and parcel of civil society and must, according to Cohen and Arato, be regarded as an important historical achievement.

But Cohen and Arato go a step further than Habermas. Recognising the imposed limitations of his view of the lifeworld, they pay more attention to patterns like self-organisation, civic associations and the public sphere, thus reworking the concept of civil society and pushing it to the boundaries. This new, critical concept of civil society not only allowed the linkage of civil activities on a horizontal level; it would also introduce a further differentiation within which it would be possible to establish and analyse vertical links. This would, as Cohen and Arato have expressed it, entail 'mediations, between individuals and groups, between groups and social institutions, and between social institutions and global political (and presumably economic) institutions or, in the case of the latter set, as an analytically separate but complementary political (and economic) society'.[8]

The concept of civil society as described above allows both a description of reality and a normative critique of that reality. Cohen and Arato are fully aware that in this respect the established democracies in Western countries are already more advanced than the new democracies of Eastern and Central Europe – not least because they are obviously more differentiated. Yet, having said this, Cohen and Arato also argue that only in contrast to and in comparison with the Eastern European experience could Western societies, and the United States in particular, become more aware of their own critical capacity.

In their account of civil society, Cohen and Arato describe the potential for change and radical rethinking in terms of the concept of civil society only in the most general terms; rarely do they refer to their own American society or to genuine American debates. It was left to such thinkers as Jeffrey C. Isaac and Jeffrey C. Goldfarb to elaborate and to apply the insights that stemmed from other, mainly Eastern European, experiences to the case of America.

The 'wake-up call' that not only reminded American intellectuals and academics of other experiences and of their own isolationist thinking but also initiated a debate about the impact these experiences had on the reformulation of American social and political thought came from Jeffrey C. Isaac. Against the self-congratulatory voices of American political scientists after 1989 and against the intellectual 'icing on the cake' from the likes of Francis Fukuyama or Samuel Huntington, who saw their case of the final victory of liberal democracy in a third wave of democratisation confirmed, Jeffrey Isaac argued that the events of 1989 should be treated differently, more as a further opportunity to democratise established democracies.[9] America should, in this respect, not be treated exceptionally. In the past the confrontation had been one between totalitarianism and democracy. In that locked-in position democracy was rarely critically investigated – not least because democracy stood out and had to be defended against the totalitarian threat. At the end of the Cold War, there is now no longer the need to follow such defensive reasoning; for there is now a chance not only to investigate the complexities of modern democracies but also to think about the further democratisation of democracy.

In his thought-provoking essay 'The Strange Silence of Political Theory' Jeffrey Isaac spells out more concretely the significance of '1989'.[10] The author reminds the academic and the wider American intellectual community that in the past revolutionary experiences had led major thinkers to reflect anew on the social and political conditions and how they shaped the perception and behaviour of individuals. Isaac lists such illustrious names as Jefferson and Madison, Paine and Wollstonecraft, Burke, Kant and Hegel, and, whereas in the past there seemed to have been an understanding of the universal dimensions of revolutionary events such as the English and French Revolutions, no such understanding can be taken for granted in American political science when it came to the events of 1989; rather 'business as usual' seemed to have been the reaction. One could summarise the lame response in questions such as: why, after all that has been before, should American democracy change? Surely the events of 1989 could be interpreted as late achievements of what American intellectuals had preached about for the past 200 years; why then change a winning, democratic team? It is this kind of laissez-faire attitude that Isaac is not prepared to accept. For him, contemporary political theory must challenge the 'canonical repository of wisdom'[11] and continue the work of the deconstruction of the 'myth of tradition' – just as the intellectual historians Quentin Skinner and John Pocock have done with their concerns with the republican ideas in what now seems a very distant past. In short, Isaac mourns the lack of proper dealings with reality. Political science, in his view, has become a self-congratulatory enterprise in which it is more important to affirm the wisdom of already existing paradigms in textbooks than to deal with that which is new and relatively unexplored. In a way Isaac himself turns out to be a Jeremiadan critic, in that he reminds the discipline of the social science of the promise that social and political thought once held. According to Isaac, the time has now come to cash in on these promises. He reminds the academic discipline further of the critique that C. Wight Mills once made, namely that it is usually the extremes of high-flying theory or empiricism that make the social sciences impotent in dealing with new events.

Yet somehow Isaac's critique remains locked into what he criticises; he seems unable to apply, in any concrete fashion, his own critique to the American reality. To be more precise, one must investigate the exact relationship between the renewed concept of civil society and American society. What is the deeper meaning of Tocqueville's insistence on the achievements of a society that governs itself and the promise of a sovereignty of the people? What implications could this have under modern conditions? It was another scholar, Jeffrey C. Goldfarb, who came to the forefront in providing answers to these questions.

Jeffrey C. Goldfarb began considering early on the lessons that could be learned from the debates of dissident circles of Eastern Europe. Having studied public life in Poland and America and *The Post-Totalitarian Mind* before it became the talk of the day, he then attempted to synthesise his work in his study *The Cynical Society*.[12] It is this study which fully explores the possibility of applying a renewed notion of civil society to American conditions.

Goldfarb commences his study with a surprising observation: although there are absolute political differences between a system based on totalitarian control and free democratic systems, it turns out that cynicism was important to the functioning of both systems. While cynicism helped the Soviet system survive, it did not contribute to overthrowing the system; in fact it rather hindered it. In the United States cynicism developed for other reasons, mainly because people were disappointed that the democratic society did not deliver what it promised, namely a comprehensive and deliberate say by its citizens on the decisions that have an impact on them.

Goldfarb sees relativism at the very root of the problem that America faces – either in the form of 'mindless patriotism', 'anticommunism' or 'truisms of simple left-right political categorisation'.[13] What can be learned from the anti-totalitarian struggles in Eastern Europe and what can cure the cynicist disease is what Goldfarb calls a 'post-totalitarian mentality'. Its main attributes are an 'anti-utopian political sensibility', and a frame of mind based on irony which knows about the 'self-limiting perspective' of its politics.[14] Goldfarb knows that American citizens are almost by nature post-totalitarian; he also reminds us that that does not mean that Americans are anti-ideological per se. Both ideology and its cure, democratic deliberation, are deeply enshrined in America's political culture. It is this discovery which also helps Goldfarb in insisting on the difference between democracy and dictatorship. While reason and power are almost indistinguishable in a totalitarian society, the same does not apply to democracies, where power and reason are not as closely linked; it is this gap which also provides the chances for developing an antidote to cynicism. Discussing the various pros and cons of critical studies such as those of C. Wright Mills and Edward Shils, Goldfarb comes to the conclusion that the actual decision-making process is not as conspiratorial as some critics (such as C.Wright Mills) have suggested and that other ideas of mass society, such as the distinction between periphery and centre (as suggested by Edward Shils), must also take various forms of participation into account, forms of participation which not infrequently lead to 'the integration of the periphery into the centre'.[15] Goldfarb insists on the fact that some mediation, mainly through the cultural sphere, does actually take place in American society. It is through such mediations in the cultural realm that a decision is made which path is being followed, that of mass society without democracy or that of democratic practices in modern mass society.

According to Goldfarb the rhetoric of cultural decline on both the Right and the Left has not helped to further the democratic process. Critics like Allan Bloom (on the right) and Russel Jacoby (on the left), instead helped cynics in their 'coming out'. Furthermore, Goldfarb doesn't find it surprising that these critics somehow have a problem in linking their discoveries to the actual state America is in. There is, in other words, no mediation taking place, and there is no American argument to be found in the critics' complacent reasoning. The further problem that results from such non-mediation between mass and democracy is that all ideas (minus some elitist classics whose reading is determined by Bloom and the likes) are being ridiculed and rendered ideological nonsense – an attitude that also enforces cynical views. If all ideas are indeed ideologies, then the best thing is to abstain from intellectual encounter altogether. As Goldfarb stresses, the long-term results of such a cynical view must simply be regarded as disastrous: since it promotes a mass culture empty of all meaningful exchange, no spread of ideas takes place and no mediation between mass and deliberate democratic decision making is possible.

In offering a solution to the problem discussed, Goldfarb relies on thoughts and ideas that predecessors like John Dewey and C. Wright Mills had voiced, insisting that only the creation of autonomous public spheres can provide an answer to the problem posed. It is the constant renewal of this public sphere, from universities to public radio, that guarantees a commodity-free exchange of ideas and public deliberation. In a passage that very much resembles Dewey and Mills, Goldfarb states that 'mass culture promotes mass society. Autonomous culture promotes the development and defence of autonomous publics. In the former, atomised individuals, separated from one another, receive messages – information, entertainment, facts and figures – from a centralised source. In the latter, individuals exchange ideas, experiences, and judgements among themselves.'[16]

As we have seen, it is the struggle for autonomous publics and for a renewed public sphere that is very much at the heart of modern civil society and which is obviously the solution to cynicism. With respect to the project of a renewal of civil society, the contribution of intellectuals is crucial. As Goldfarb states in his follow-up study *Civility and Subversion – The Intellectual in Democratic Society* it is the task of intellectuals to 'facilitate public deliberations about problems buried by the norms of civility'.[17] The very way in which intellectuals can 'cultivate civility' is through 'the subversion of restrictive common sense'.[18] The main problem that a renewed concept of civil society in western societies – particularly the US – faces is, however, that of a 'deliberation deficit', that is, it is less a problem of access to information than a question of informed discussion.

Where exactly is informed discussion taking place in the modern public sphere? According to Goldfarb various intellectuals have tried to provide an answer. For John Dewey and Walter Lippman the answer lay in an enlightened public. In Lippman's case it should rely on experts knowledge, a rather technocratic solution, while in Dewey's case education is supposed to contribute to the resuscitation of public life. For Goldfarb, Lippman addressed the elite while Dewey sought alliance with the enlightened crowds. In contrast to such 'elitist' and 'talkative' solutions, other attempts, which Goldfarb calls 'shouting attempts', differed in their approach to reason in public. The most prominent representatives of such public deliberation were, again, C. Wright Mills and, more recently, Edward Said. Mills appears to be the radicalisation of Dewey in that he sympathises with the idea of the re-emergence of the public but has doubts about the role education plays. For him it is rather the new cultural worker who reminds the public of the fact of undemocratic history-making. At the same time Mills does not provide a definitive answer to the problem of the role of the intellectual workman. Too many doubts remain about the future success of the new intellectual – not least because the transformation from former local publics into a mass society was so prevalent. Furthermore, Mills doubted whether American intellectuals would be prepared to speak the 'American language'.

Edward Said, a Palestinian scholar who in the course of the 1980s and 1990s has become one of the most prominent public intellectuals on American campuses, disagrees with Mills. He shows that the intellectual is also a group member; he is not alone – and thus has to take sides. For Said, the intellectual as a group member has to speak the truth. He is either 'part of the problem or part of the solution'.[19] Countering Said, Goldfarb is right in stressing that this position often leads to the creation of philosopher kings – on both sides of the conflict, either on the side of the oppressed or on the side of the oppressor. The result can be disastrous and, while Said is right in stressing the commitment to the oppressed, which is often an ethnic group and/or a minority group, the problem becomes obvious when multiculturalism turns into 'multitribalism' (Goldfarb). To preach to the already converted – as Noam Chomsky and others do – does nothing for the resuscitation of the public sphere and the furtherance of civil society. As Goldfarb stresses, intellectuals 'provide democracies with their political vocabularies';[20] and in an environment like the US this becomes increasingly problematic. Goldfarb cites the example of the universities where two tendencies are at work: on one side institutions of higher education certainly provide a safe haven and net for free speech and deliberation; on the other side a division of labour develops whereby the public at large remains unaffected by the arguments provided by academics and intellectuals. The result is problematic: the contemporary American university emerges as an intellectual reserve that only occasionally communicates with the outside world – and even then it does so in a way that the broader public is not able to assimilate, because the specialist language or political rhetoric becomes untranslatable.

Having said that, provoking thoughts and subversity often serves to advance situations, yet it is not quite enough, and can often turn into mere entertainment if prolonged. The aim therefore must be to find the time and space for democratic deliberation, with civility being both a precondition and a result from such deliberation. In this last respect, Goldfarb's study can only hint at possible solutions. Whether this will help to further the development of civil society remains open.

Some of the most important contributions to the discussion of the relationship between civil society, social theory and the task of intellectuals have come from feminists. The first American account that is now regarded as a modern classic was *Public Man, Private Woman – Women in Social and Political Thought* by Jean Bethke Elshtain.[21] In the first part of her study Elshtain prepared the ground and showed that throughout history and indeed throughout the history of social and political thought, from Aristotle through to Marx, women have consistently been confined to the private sphere. The second part of the study deals with various women's responses to the problem; it is this part in particular that is relevant to our discussion. In her discussion Elshtain makes a distinction between four standpoints within the feminists' search for politics: radical, liberal, Marxist and psychoanalytic feminism. Radical feminism can be summarised under the heading of 'the personal is political'. It is suggested that since public life served as a means to repress women and the private life used to confine women, upholding the distinction of private and public between the two spheres makes little sense in terms of an emancipatory programme. Nothing personal should be separated; rather everything that relates to the personal must be seen as political. As Elshtain suggests: 'There is a total collapse of public and private as central categories of explanation or description.'[22] The author concludes that 'if there are no distinctions between public and private, personal and political, it follows that no differentiated activity or set of institutions that are genuinely political, that are, in fact, the bases of order and of purpose in a political community, exist.'[23] The danger that Elshtain sees in such an attitude is a thorough anti-intellectualism. Indeed any intellectual effort is in danger of being suspected to be male, or at least male-oriented – with the dubious result that the 'male mind'–'female emotion' distinction becomes essentialised.

Liberal feminism in contrast assumes that a distinction between public and private should be upheld – although in the modified form, so that more women can enter and participate in the public realm. Political power structures are assumed to function properly as long as they admit an equal number of women. Yet, as Elshtain points out, what was genuinely male about social and political institutions was rarely questioned. Furthermore, the ends of politics are accepted unequivocally. Thus the emancipatory project is limited to the classic liberal and middle-class-based programme of 'individualism, self-interest, (and) role changing'.[24] Marxist feminism questions exactly this and asks women to see the links between the exploitation of the proletariat and the suppression of women. Yet according to Elshtain this perspective fails to see what was specific about the repression of women; Marxist feminism prefers not to differentiate and lumps all kinds of exploitation together. Reproduction as a preliminary stage to production in general is thus the only genuine contribution of Marxist feminism to the overall discussion of where the feminist political project is going. Against the Marxist objectivist view of exploitation the subjective turn of psycho-analytic-based feminism seems to be the appropriate answer and, as Elshtain maintains, is promising answers to the problem posed. Psychoanalytic feminism seems to be stronger in its differentiated view of gendered identities and in its insistence on keeping the public and private sphere separate – although not unchanged or unreformed (not least because stronger women's identities can change both sides from within, almost in terms of a 'politics of subjectivity').

In her own response the author's argument is less impressive and falls somehow short of the highly differentiated views she put to the reader when dealing with the earlier critique of the social and political thought classics and in her treatment of contemporary streams of feminism. To insist that public space per se can be neglected and to talk about the 'iron cage of the agora'[25] seems to diminish any expression of republican ideas. In particular, Elshtain's emphasis on and defence of motherhood and maternal thinking as the crucial, distinctive dimension has been criticised. Feminist thinkers such as Mary Dietz, Seyla Benhabib and Joan B. Landes [26] took particular issue with how the public sphere and women's emancipation could be linked; theirs are contributions that either explicitly or implicitly challenge Elshtain's views.

Dietz asks why, when all that feminists demand for motherhood and the social practices associated with it has been met, women still question why they have been left out of the male-dominated democratic discourse. The point that Dietz tries to make is poignantly summarised in the statement that '(good) mothers may also be (good) citizens, but their being (good) mothers does not make them (good) citizens'.[27] Dietz also reminds Elshtain that in modern democracy and in modern citizenship individuals are regarded as being equal. In this repect 'the mother-child relationship is a particularly inappropriate model'.[28] Dietz' resolution – directed against Elshtain – is that the feminist movement must not speak the language of 'love and compassion, but only the language of freedom, equality, citizenship, and justice'.[29] Against the particularistic notion of motherhood and maternal thinking Dietz insists that feminism must develop a more comprehensive view in which the question of the universal dimensions of citizenship needs particularly to be addressed – otherwise feminist discourse will always be always limited to addressing only 50 per cent of human kind.[30]

Seyla Benhabib aims her criticism at the fact that most of the important contributions to the theorising of the public sphere (Habermas, Arendt) fail to account for the all too obvious gender differences; she refers in particular to the dimensions of the private spheres which, to a large extent, provide the material basis for entering and being successful within the public sphere.[31] It seems that in this respect Benhabib would sympathise with the attention that Elshtain pays to the 'material' conditions of motherhood. Yet Benhabib also sees the benefits in using republican means for feminist ends – this becomes particularly clear in her defence of public discourse and the public sphere as a means to question male-dominated power structures in the public and private realm.

Joan B. Landes agrees with this critique but counters Benhabib on how radical the changes will have to be.[32] Against the partial dismissal of such a thinker as Hannah Arendt, Landes stresses that one thing that can be learned from Arendt is her emphasis on the weak position of individuals and that such neglected subjective dimensions as storytelling could empower female individuals entering the public realm.

Yet all in all Dietz, Benhabib and Landes, in their critiques, all remain somehow abstract – which cannot be said about Mary P. Ryan's contribution to the debate. Her pertinent account of how women in nineteenth-century America participated in various political causes, and thus not only left traces but also transformed the public sphere itself, stands for a significant shift in perspective.[33] It challenges the assumption of many feminist critics – particularly those who engage with the Habermasian view of a steady decline of the public bourgeois sphere – and challenges feminist views that over-whelmingly seem to see women as victims. Against such a perspective Ryan's analysis illustrates the fact that it makes little sense to treat the public sphere as a social realm with strictly defined partitions. Formerly marginalised groups and social protests that are progressive may well come in 'from the dark' and see in the due course of time the bright light of the public sphere. This in turn can lead to the further securing of rights – rights that have been thus far neglected. Ryan adds that to defend one's particular interests can also have a universal dimension and lead to the 'public good'. Thus, although she never refers directly to the rhetoric of the Jeremiad, Ryan reveals that the Jeremiad is not simply a male discourse. Ryan not only reminds the reader that long neglected feminist politics can indeed have the structure of and pursue the path of the American Jeremiad; she also makes clear that social theory, civil society and the task of intellectuals are intrinsically linked to and indeed benefit from all levels of such feminist inheritance.[34]

Notes

1. *Making History – The American Left and the American Mind* (New York: Columbia University Press 1988).
2. Flacks' account can also be read as an attempt to spell out where the Left had gone wrong in the past – particularly when (in an attempt to democratise history-making) it imported concepts from abroad (be it from the former Soviet Union, China or Vietnam) and forgot about American values such as the pragmatically oriented 'making history to make life'.

3. *Making History*, p. 43.
4. Ibid. p. 43.
5. Ibid. p. 286.
6. Norman Podhoretz, David Horowitz and Daniel Bell are all connected to the ideas of Neoconservatism and/or Neoliberalism, a line of thought that abhors totalitarianism in thought and practice for all the right reasons but that is at the same time inclined to defend the capitalist status quo because it is the means that favours individual choice and the market. It is probably fair to say that their intellectual mentor is the Robert Nozick of *Anarchy, State and Utopia*. The Neo-liberal and Neo-conservative approaches became prominent when their main representatives mixed with politics and became powerful. Their political anthropology, which sees the individual as the prime actor who needs to be freed from all social constraints, was later challenged by the communitarians, who, as the name suggests, saw the relationship between the individual and society mediated through belonging to one or more community. Both intellectual groupings received widespread attention − not least because their 'programmes' were linked to influential power politics. Whether neoliberalism and communitarians ever constituted more than fashionable tendencies within the American intellectual tradition remains to historians to judge. I, however, have some doubts − not least because the two approaches consist of such heterogeneous elements that to place them all together under one label serves little purpose.
7. Jean Cohen and Andrew Arato: *Civil Society and Political Theory* (Cambridge, MA: MIT Press 1992).
8. Ibid. p. 478.
9. Jeffrey C. Isaac: *Democracy in Dark Times* (Ithaca/London: Cornell University Press 1998).
10. 'The Strange Silence of Political Theory' in: ibid.
11. Ibid. p. 48.
12. *On Cultural Freedom − Public Life in Poland and in America* (Chicago/London: The University of Chicago Press 1982); *Beyond Glasnost: The Post-Totalitarian Mind* (Chicago: University of Chicago Press 1989); *The Cynical Society* (Chicago/London: The University of Chicago Press 1991).
13. *The Cynical Society*, p. 11.
14. All quotes from ibid. p. 11.
15. Ibid. p. 45.
16. Ibid. p. 144.
17. *Civility and Subversion* (Cambridge: Cambridge University Press 1998). The quote is from p. 1.
18. Ibid. p. 1.
19. Ibid. p. 69.
20. Ibid. p. 81.
21. *Public Man − Private Woman* (Princeton, NJ: Princeton University Press 1981). A further elaboration of the original argument can be found in the essay

'Antigone's Daughter', originally published in *Democracy in the World*, 2/2 (1982), pp. 46–59.

22. *Public Man – Private Woman*, p. 217.
23. Ibid.
24. Ibid. p. 247.
25. Ibid. p. 348.
26. Some of these publications are not readily accessible. Two volumes in particular, *Feminism – The Public and The Private* (ed. Joan B. Landes, Oxford/New York: Oxford University Press 1998) and *Feminism and Politics* (ed. Anne Phillips, Oxford/New York: Oxford University Press 1998), now make it easier to consider the debates in comprehensive volumes. Furthermore, both readers focus mainly on American debates – thereby signifying that the intellectual debate in the United States is more advanced compared to anywhere else. For further references I will refer to the reprinted texts in these two volumes.
27. 'Citizenship with a Feminist Face: The Problem with Maternal Thinking' originally published in *Political Theory*, 13/1 (Feb. 1985): 19–37, reprinted in *Feminism – The Public and the Private*, pp. 45–64. The quote is from p. 57.
28. Ibid. p. 58.
29. Ibid. p. 61.
30. See also Mary G. Dietz's 'Context Is All: Feminism and Theories of Citizenship', originally published in *Daedalus* 116/4 (Fall 1987), reprinted in *Feminism and Politics*, pp. 378–400.
31. 'Models of Public Space: Hannah Arendt, the Liberal Tradition, and Jürgen Habermas' was originally published in *Habermas and the Public Sphere* (ed. Craig Calhoun, Cambridge, MA: MIT Press 1992, pp. 72–98) and is reprented in *Feminism – The Public and The Private*, pp. 65–99.
32. 'The Public and the Private Sphere' originally in *Feminists Read Habermas: Gendering the Subject of Discourse* (New York: Routledge 1995), reprinted in *Feminism – The Public and the Private*, pp. 135–63.
33. 'Gender and Public Access: Women's Politics in Nineteenth-Century America' originally published in *Habermas and the Public Sphere* (ed. Craig Calhoun, Cambridge, MA: MIT Press 1992), pp. 259–88, reprinted in *Feminism – The Public and the Private*, pp. 195–222.

Chapter 10

American Social and Political Thought at the Dawn of the Twenty-first Century

Michael Sandel's synthesising efforts to renew public philosophy ● Thinking the good society: means-centred procedural liberalism versus ends-oriented formative republicanism ● The response of liberals and pluralists to Sandel's critique: Nancy Rosenblum, Richard Rorty, Richard Sennett, Charles Taylor and Michael Walzer ● New on the agenda: 'epistemological democracy' ● The moral dimension of the social sciences: from the mere critique of Jean Bethke Elshtain and Christopher Beem to the conceptualisation of the 'economy of morals' through Albert O. Hirschman and Alan Wolfe ● Reprise: the role of the intellectual in the liberal republic

Facing the dawn of the twenty-first century offers an opportunity to look both to the past and to the future. Michael J. Sandel's *Democracy's Discontent – America in Search of a Public Philosophy* is such a comprehensive account. Sandel attempts to consolidate ideas by reviewing what has gone before and anticipating the new perspectives and promise that American social and political thought might hold for the future.[1]

Sandel first tackles the prevalent wave of discontent amongst Americans dissatisfied with their current situation. This sense of discontent has its roots in the way they are governed and the way in which their institutions are run, compounded by a growing critical awareness of the chasm that had opened up between those who govern and those who are governed. Indeed, the sense of discontent seems to have spread into all aspects of civic life. There is not only a deep mistrust of governmental institutions, but the widening malaise stands to threaten the very moral fabric of community life. Sandel attributes the main source of this discontent to the political philosophy of the day – that of liberalism. Sandel, who recognises that both republicanism and liberalism have played instrumental roles in the shaping of American democracy, is quick to point out that liberalism has taken the dominant role for more than the last hundred years. Having said that, Sandel does not tag liberalism a one-sided coin and freely admits its compound aspects. In particular, he distinguishes between egalitarian liberals who are in favour of the welfare state and civil rights, and libertarian liberals who fear the distributive mechanisms supported by the former, and are more likely to put up a strong defence for the market economy.

Sandel states that, independent of such differential views within liberalism, a fundamental flaw remains at the very root of liberal ideas – a flaw which he identifies as a 'political anthropology,' which has the tendency to view individuals as utterly self-seeking monads pursuing selfish aims. Sandel further points out that the narrow view of liberalism fails to recognise that there are other inherent other factors at play, factors such as commitment, loyalty and responsibility. Without crediting the role of these factors and indeed promoting them, modern society will continue to be increasingly effected by a sense of discontent.

The real danger lies especially in the fact that a viewpoint that regards individuals as self-serving will naturally shape institutions along the same lines of reasoning. To counter this, Sandel proposes the revival of republican ideas that had led America in its early days. In particular he emphasises two key ideas: First, the idea of the good society (which he identifies as the aim of the self-governing republic). The aim of reviving this idea is to cultivate the republic's citizens in a culture where rights are not simply demanded and existing preferences are not blindly followed, as the liberals would have it. Second, Sandel promotes the idea of how liberty relates to self-government. Here republicans see liberty as resulting from civic virtue; that is, liberty is not just 'out there' to be protected or enhanced but rather becomes intrinsically linked to the idea of self-government. As Sandel points out: 'The liberal begins by asking how government should treat its citizens, and seeks principles of justice that treat persons fairly as they pursue their various interests and ends. The republican begins by asking how citizens can be capable of self-government, and seeks the political forms and social conditions that promote its meaningful exercise.'[2]

The whole of American history can, according to Sandel, be interpreted as a struggle between a liberal procedural republic, with an emphasis on rights, that is means–centred and a republican formative project that, with its emphasis on the good life is ends–centred. In America's past both views have struggled with each other. Thus, the early debates over the Constitution were marked by the struggle over the ideas of rights and liberties – with the favourable outcome for liberalism, maintaining that if the 'constitution is neutral among ends' the state has to remain neutral as well.[3] Another early victory for the liberal procedural republic counted on the fact that the principle of neutrality prevailed when applied to the freedom of speech –

with the result that the importance of the good argument as a precondition for civic life was diminished. As arguments were being formally treated as equal, they also had to be protected equally – with the result that all kinds of arguments, however wide of the margin, were entitled to the same right. This curtailed meaningful deliberation in public life and limited it more to a debate not for the common citizen but rather for the courtrooms.

The liberalism of the procedural republic was not only problematic when it came to constitutionalism. It also had implications for those realms of social and economic life that are not narrowly defined by strict set rules. Sandel points towards the crucial debates surrounding the ideas of work, that is, the political economy of citizenship. Republican connotations of work maintain that it is of utmost importance that work and its results should help to contribute to civic virtue, i.e. work should be a means to the ends of being virtuous. Thus republican political economy favoured the acquisition of land and the right for every citizen to benefit from independently working this land, thus guaranteeing that every citizen had the material means to fully participate in civic life. The same argument was made over manufacturing: 'The advocates of American manufactures, like the early opponents, made their case in the name of liberty and virtue, not economic growth.'[4] And even the early debates on the dubious benefits of factory life and dependent work had to answer republican questions of exactly what was so virtuous about the new way of production. It was not by chance that large parts of the labour movement still articulated their demands in the republican terms of 'free labour' against 'wage labour'. Organisations like the *Knights of Labor* and the *International Workers of the World* stood for this republican-inspired approach to free labour.

Furthermore, the insistence on functioning communities that could revive the public sphere (as Dewey had suggested), the struggle against trusts, the progressive movement – they can all be interpreted as (declining) struggles for civic virtue. Their struggle shows that even though the liberal procedural republic was on the winning side and became the hegemonic public philosophy, republican ideas still formed a strong undercurrent up until the New Deal. The New Deal (artificially prolonged through World War II and then the Cold War) ensured that 'the political economy of growth and distributive justice displaced the political economy of citizenship'.[5] Liberalism had finally won and Keynesianism had helped it to win. The consequences were problematic: first, the functioning of Keynesianism made sure that questions about the good life were postponed; second, Keynesianism also guaranteed that citizens had less choice and less voice than ever before. In the long run the consequences were disastrous for the republican idea of a formative republic; as a political project it had to be abandoned indefinitely.

Yet the liberal proceduralist project also created problems – because of its success. Seeing the liberal project thriving, citizens also began to ask questions: why is it that some American citizens are still not living the good life despite all the material wealth? Why are we seeing more and more disintegrating aspects within American society? Why are American citizens so discontented with public life? To be sure, liberals have tried to find an answer to these questions – from Johnson's practical Great Society programmes to theoretically sophisticated political philosophers such as Rawls and Nozick (the former from an egalitarian liberal position, the latter from a libertarian liberal position). Both, the practical as well as the theoretical, answers failed, mainly because the debates remained in what Sandel has called 'the voluntarist conception of freedom', a perception that does not consider the appropriate ends and how these ends can be achieved. It appeals only to the good will of citizens but does not by any means ensure that deliberation towards certain ends takes place. For Sandel this is 'the loss of mastery'.[6]

Yet with all the critique of procedural liberalism, Sandel also knows that a republican formative project has to find answers to the level of differentiation, the complexity of identity formation processes and the internationalisation that marks contemporary America. Sandel asks how 'the civic strand of freedom' can prevail under these conditions and finds an answer in the federalist tradition of America. As Sandel rightly stresses, the United States has never been a nation-state in the European sense of the word. For the US it would thus not be such a huge step to acknowledge that self-government can only work in a decentralised fashion.

Sandel reminds us also that – against the abstract universalism of the liberal project – the strength of republicanism has always been to insist on the particularity of our lives. The 'places and stories, memories and meanings, incidents and identities, that situate us in the world'.[7] Yet more than this seems necessary: a formative republican project must come to terms with moral conflict and arguments. If there is one crucial lesson to be learned from the procedural republic, it is that to 'banish moral and religious argument from political discourse makes for an impoverished civic life'.[8] A renewed republican project, Sandel maintains, would be an important step to fight both procedural liberals as well as narrow-minded conservative republicans; in short, all those 'who would banish ambiguity, shore up borders, harden the distinction between insiders and outsiders' and those who want citizens to become 'formless, protean, storyless selves, unable to weave the various strands of their identity into a coherent whole'.[9]

Sandel's critique triggered wide-ranging responses not only from liberals, but from the entire spectrum of American social and political thought.

An explanation for why Sandel's study received such a reaction is surely that Sandel's view was not of the pure republican type. As the political scientist Nancy L. Rosenblum has pointed out (in a collection devoted to the discussion of *Democracy's Discontent*), Sandel's position can be described as that of 'Fusion Republicanism'.[10] This consists of a mixture of 'democratic ideology, potential militancy, and invocation of civic virtue prevalent in American political life'.[11] It is not a consistent approach, but rather 'a conglomeration of disparate elements of political thought and practice that coalesce around certain unifying themes'.[12] It seems exactly this element of fusion that initiated a response from all sides of the political spectrum. Nevertheless, even 'Fusion Republicanism' is still republicanism, and it is not by chance that this kind of theorising aroused responses particularly from the liberal Left. In what follows, I would like to be selective and pick out only a few responses – those that deal with the idea of liberal republicanism and the ones that try to conceptualise difference in modern America. Dealing with Sandel and the responses his study triggered, I will conclude with one statement that stands out mainly because it identified a larger problem of American social and political thought – that of 'demo-cratic epistemology'.

The philosopher Richard Rorty, a self-declared 'minimalist liberal', was the critic who was most uncompromising in his discussion of *Democracy's Discontent*.[13] Rorty's response to Sandel consisted of an outright rejection of Sandel's ideas. In particular he rejected the idea that America is searching for a public philosophy. Being a democratic thinker, he questions whether philosophers can actually maintain that America is searching for a new philosophy. After all, who are these thinkers to dictate to the American public? Rorty, the pragmatist, further rejects the idea of finding answers to the big questions concerning general ideas and accounts of liberty or freedom. To be more specific, he questions whether Sandel is clear about the *political* meaning of the word liberty – the only meaning that gives liberty a concrete dimension in the American republic. What else, asks Rorty, can one do to improve deliberations on liberty, than to provide 'more reflective people' through 'education, security and leisure . . . They are more patient, tolerant, and imaginative, and so are better citizens of a democracy'.[14] This, Rorty maintains, would be his first minimalist liberal answer to Sandel's republican project of a formative republic.

But Rorty also rejects Sandel's notion of truth; it is here that he is arguing on pragmatist grounds. Rorty reminds Sandel of the fact that one of the great truths about political liberalism is that it has learned how to deal with uncompromising illiberal or extreme views. In Rorty's view, it is not the formative republic that helps here, but the liberal pragmatist attitude, which consists of better education of the citizenry, to teach 'the civic virtue of having as few such compelling interests, beliefs, and desires as possible'.[15] In the end Rorty turns out not only to be a democrat and a pragmatist but also an old-fashioned leftist in that he questions whether the emphasis that Sandel's republican thought pays to ideas like the ones of 'the loss of agency' and disempowerment is not really due to banal political and social tendencies, such as the increasing power of the American oligarchy, and the increasing social and cultural gap between this oligarchy and the rest of the American people.

Richard Sennett, one of the most prominent American sociologists, interprets the debate between Sandel and Rorty as a debate of 'Two Models of the Republic', between one model that is based on a restrictive version of citizenship (the liberal model) and another model which is once again interested in civic duty and loyalty (the republican model).[16] The two models revolve around the question of how one defines the relationship between civil society and political activity. Obviously Sandel's approach favours a strong relationship between the two. Thus the study itself can be understood as a contribution to the stirring up of public debate and as an attempt to resuscitate 'the politics of commitment' (Sennett) – with the intention of strengthening the links between civil society and political activity. With this Rorty couldn't disagree more. He abhors a view that sees 'political activity as cathartic' (Sennett) – not only because of potential misuse, but also because of its strong value-laden rhetoric.

A second important set of responses to Sandel came from pluralists, multiculturalists and communitarian thinkers such as Michael Walzer and Charles Taylor. Walzer is in overall agreement with a social criticism that sees an underlying potential for improvement within the same society that is criticised, yet he questions the one-sidedness of Sandel's historical account – particularly when it comes to the history of pluralism.[17] Walzer maintains that there are two forms of communitarian deliberation, one in which civic republicanism is being regarded as stemming from a view that sees the entire country as one community, and another one that is more pluralist in that the country is regarded as a community consisting of other communities, 'a whole constituted by its parts'.[18] For Walzer, Sandel's view is one-sided and discusses only the first form of possible deliberation. It only deals superficially with the history of migration which, according to Walzer, made American society what it is today (namely different from other republics on this globe). To neglect the relationship between the two communitarian forms neglects a constitutional part of a country where immigrants have made a difference – 'a difference that requires philosophical as well as practical acknowledgement'.[19] The Canadian philosopher Charles Taylor is in line with Walzer's reasoning. In his response to Sandel he agrees with the overall purpose and intention of the book – namely to think again publicly of the aim and purpose of society; yet he also questions whether the formative republic regards 'difference' as substantially important. In Sandel, as in much of contemporary philosophy, Taylor misses 'models of how people can associate and be bonded together in difference, without abstracting from these differences'.[20] Taylor even radicalises this question and takes it a step further: can we think of a model where differences can actually contribute to deliberation in a formative republic? Can difference enrich social life? And finally and most crucially: could it not be that people bond not despite the differences but as a result of those very differences? Here liberalism has few answers; as a matter of fact, procedural liberalism shies away from the problems concerned with difference – not least because it would have to abstract from all differences in order to make the model applicable to all. With respect to these problems, Taylor maintains that the republicanism of Sandel is superior as it once again throws open the question of the aim, the *telos* of the entire enterprise called society. Yet it also must be said that for Taylor, Sandel's formative republicanism does not go far enough. For Taylor and the communitarian approach the question of 'how to live as equals in difference' (Taylor) remains unanswered in Sandel's vision of the formative republican project.

Sandel has responded to the criticisms of both the liberals and the pluralists.[21] In his response to the liberals and in particular to Rorty he questions how far liberals are true to their own liberal and pragmatic tradition. After all, was it not John Dewey who wrote *The Public and its Problems* – a book that surely qualifies as public philosophy and a book that also talked about values and deliberation?

Concerning the criticism voiced by the pluralists, Sandel agrees that diversity poses a challenge to a republican project. Yet he also states that the advantage of discussing diversity in the context of a formative republic is also that the problem is no longer limited to the question of who gets what and why, but also about the way things are being produced and how we work. It seemed as if the political economy of citizenship ought to remain the strongest point in Sandel's account.

It is regrettable that Sandel had almost nothing to say about a point that has been made by two other critics, Jean Bethke Elshtain and Christopher Beem. In their assessment of Sandel's contribution they had hinted at a point that not only Sandel but other theorists rarely reflect upon – the notion of democratic epistemology.[22] With the term 'democratic epistemology' Elshtain and Beem referred to the problem that something such as civic virtue can only be understood and conceptualised if it is 'out there'.

Unfortunately Elshtain and Beem did not themselves develop this point any further, but rather left us with a remark which potentially represents an entire programme, namely that of coming up with concepts that would allow the social scientist to both describe the actual state of civil society and to identify the democratic potential of civil society that lies behind the status quo. However, research into this field has been conducted by two other prominent American thinkers, Albert O. Hirschman and Alan Wolfe.

Albert O. Hirschman in his critique of political economy was not the first to trespass academic boundaries, yet he was the first one to tackle the challenge and the idea of democratic epistemology seriously. He first studied the moral foundations of political economy in his groundbreaking study *The Passions and the Interests*.[23] His findings – namely, that we do not stop being human beings who have moral considerations and make moral choices when we enter the market or when we labour – are then applied to social realms other than the market in *Exit, Voice and Loyalty*.[24] In *Shifting Involvements* he goes a step further in attempting to concretise the application to the realms of private and public life and the relationship between the two.[25] In *The Rhetoric of Reaction* he then deconstructed the conservative rhetoric and the ideology of economistic thinking in politics.[26]

What makes Hirschman's thinking different in terms of epistemological democracy is that his concepts have both a normative and a descriptive element. Concepts such as 'exit', 'voice', 'loyalty' lead to thinking along the lines of 'nibbling' and 'possibilism', allowing the social scientist to investigate both the normative dimensions of civil society and the actual, existing civil society – with the gap between the two indicating the potential for further democratisation.

The sociologist Alan Wolfe's reasoning resembles that of Hirschman. In his critical account of the social sciences in *Whose Keeper?* he reflects upon the relationship between social science and moral obligation and thus takes us a step further even than Hirschman. He assesses the market, the state and society and investigates what connects the three related disciplines of economics, political science and sociology when it comes to moral questions.[27] His conclusion of the academic division of labour and the state of the three social science disciplines could not be more revealing. In particular capitalist economics and liberal political science seem to have lost sight of why they were 'invented' in the first place. Presenting themselves now as disciplines that pretend to study the market and the state, they de facto are responsible for promising citizens 'freedom from economics and liberation from politics'.[28] Thus they have gone a long way from a political economy which was once a morally motivated enterprise promoting the advancement of civil society – not least through the virtuous participation of each citizen. Against the anti-moral stand and decay of both political science and economics, Wolfe seeks to revitalise the idea of civil society. It is the social world of civil society that provides the social foundation upon which state and the market can develop and thrive – yet this is forgotten, not least because the concepts with which both economics and political science operate are very limited and do not explain the social preconditions of both the market and the state. The danger is thus the continuous 'withering away of civil society'.[29] Against this, Wolfe aims at restoring the balance. Yet to do this, sociology must also open itself up to new ways of thinking by introducing concepts that reflect the moral choices that citizens make each day. Like Hirschman, Wolfe wants the social scientist to think about 'exit' and 'voice'; but against the neglect of the concept of 'loyalty' in Hirschman – which originally figured prominently in his work – he asks the social scientist to re-focus on this neglected concept. Wolfe thus reminds Hirschman (and other social scientists) of his own, famous saying, namely that it is loyalty that holds exit at bay and allows voice to thrive. Furthermore, in order to find out how exactly loyalty functions, social scientists should focus more on the investigation of the 'entrance', 'waiting' and 'exit' rules of civil society.

What Wolfe hints at is nothing more than the relationship that exists between a democratic society and the theoretical democratisation of the social sciences. A reciprocity between the two can only emerge if the social sciences become truly democratic in re-adjusting the ends, that is the idea of the good and democratic society, to the appropriate means, that is, conceptual understanding. Only then will it be once again justified to speak of the social sciences as a moral enterprise.

The question of how to understand democratic epistemology and democratic concepts leads us to our last quest – that of the positioning of the thinker and intellectual in a modern democracy. Where exactly do they stand in a democratic society, and what role are they able to play as citizens?

Michael Walzer has tried to answer these questions by stressing that only those intellectuals who hold the balance between attachment and detachment have been and possibly will be in a position not only to criticise society but also to be read and heard by a wider audience.[30] Having made this general point, it of course then depends on the individual circumstances: in a dictatorship it is nonsensical to feel attached to the prevailing uncivil society and exit might prove to be the only option. In democracies, the issue is more complicated, as one can raise one's voice only if one also shows some loyalty to the democratic society that one belongs to.

Richard Rorty has elaborated on Walzer's point. What remains for the intellectual within a liberal society is to use the tools of irony. Yet Rorty goes a step further even. In his radical pragmatist view, democracy and democratic ideas and practices should reign supreme when it comes to philosophy. Rorty here incorporates the lesson from the totalitarian inclinations of so many philosophic thinkers and theorists. In terms of conflicting values between philosophic absolute claims of truth and democratic arrangements, it is always the latter that should prevail.[31]

It is appropriate at this point to finally introduce C.L.R. James – a thinker who represents, as a Tocquevillean Marxist, the ultimate combination of a European-American intellectual enterprise. In his study of *American Civilisation*, C.L.R. James made it clear – quite some time before Walzer and Rorty arrived on the scene – that he regarded American intellectuals as a breed apart from their counterparts in Europe: 'Because of the peculiarly free conditions of democracy in the United States, the American intellectuals as a social group were the first to face as a practical question the beginnings of a problem which has been fully recognised during the last twenty years – the relation of individualism to democracy as a whole; while in Europe the question was narrowed and at the same time concretised by all sorts of special conditions.'[32] What C.L.R. James hints at here, is what distinguishes the American intellectual from the European intellectual – his predisposition to democracy and the way in which individual expression is intrinsically linked to modern American civil society. This is a fact that is also deeply imbued into the writing process of intellectuals, as C.L.R. James particularly demonstrates in the work of Herman Melville.[33] Falling short of a radical expression such as the *Communist Manifesto*, for James the work of Melville almost becomes the intellectual equivalent of such a manifesto. In his interpretation of Melville's work he points out that individual expression must always be seen in the context of the development of modern mass society. Stressing again the difference from Europe he writes: 'European bourgeois culture, so remarkable in its day, is today an incubus, a weight, an obstacle. The American people, the great body of them, are ignorant of many things their European brothers know. But in social culture, technical knowledge, sense of equality, the instinct for social co-operation and collective life, the need to live a full life in every sphere and a revulsion to submission, to accepting a social situation is insoluble, they are the most highly civilised people on the face of the globe. They combine an excessive individualism, a sense of the primary value of their own individual personality, with an equally remarkable need, desire and capacity for social co-operative action. And when you consider the immense millions of them, they constitute a social force such as the world has never seen before. Their power has been seen only in snatches so far.'[34]

It is in paragraphs like this one that C.L.R. James hints at the democratic withering of intellectuals as a separate class – a very democratic manifesto indeed.

Notes

1. *Democracy's Discontent – America in Search of a Public Philosophy* (Cambridge, MA: Harvard University Press 1996).
2. Ibid. p. 27.
3. Ibid. p. 46.
4. Ibid. p. 142.
5. Ibid. p. 250.
6. Ibid. p. 294.
7. Ibid. p. 349.
8. Ibid. p. 349.
9. Ibid. p. 350.
10. Nancy L. Rosenblum: 'Fusion Republicanism' in: Anita L. Allen and Milton C. Regan, Jr: Debating Democracy's Discontent (Oxford/New York: Oxford University Press 1998), pp. 273–88.
11. Ibid. p. 273.
12. Ibid. p. 273.
13. Richard Rorty: 'A Defense of Minimalist Liberalism' in: Allen and Regan: *Debating Democracy's Discontent*, pp. 117–25.
14. Ibid. p. 119.
15. Ibid. p. 120.
16. Richard Sennett: 'Two Models of the Republic' in: Allen/Regan: *Debating Democracy's Discontent*, pp. 126–30.
17. Michael Walzer: 'Michael Sandel's America' in: Allen/Regan: *Debating Democracy's Discontent*, pp. 175–82.
18. Ibid. p. 175.
19. Ibid. p. 182.
20. Charles Taylor: 'Living with Difference' in: Allen/Regan: *Debating Democracy's Discontent*, pp. 212–26. The quote is from p. 214.
21. Michael Sandel: 'Reply to Critics' in: Allen/Regan: *Debating Democracy's Discontent*, pp. 319–35.
22. Jean Bethke Elshtain and Christopher Beem: 'Can This Republic Be Saved?' in: Allen/Regan: *Debating Democracy's Discontent*, pp. 193–204. The term democratic-epistemology only appears at the end of the essay on p. 204.
23. Albert O. Hirschman: *The Passions and the Interests* (Princeton, NJ: Princeton University Press 1977).
24. *Exit, Voice, and Loyalty* (Cambridge, MA: Harvard University Press 1970).

25. *Shifting Involvements. Private Interest and Public Action* (Princeton, NJ: Princeton University Press 1982).
26. *The Rhetoric of Reaction* (Cambridge, MA: Belknap Press of Harvard University Press).
27. Alan Wolfe: *Whose Keeper? Social Science and Moral Obligation* (Berkeley/Los Angeles: University of California Press 1989).
28. Ibid. p. 1.
29. Ibid. p. 14.
30. Michael Walzer: *Interpretation and Social Criticism* (Cambridge, MA: Harvard University Press 1987). In *The Company of Critics* (New York: Basic Books 1988) Walzer elaborates on ideas first presented in *Interpretation and Social Criticism*.
31. See Richard Rorty: *Contingency, Irony, and Solidarity* (Cambridge: Cambridge University Press 1989) and his essay 'The Priority of Democracy to Philosophy' in: Solidarität oder Objektivität? (Stuttgart: Reclam 1988); pp. 82–125.
32. C.L.R. James: *American Civilization* (Cambridge, MA/Oxford: Blackwell 1993) p. 50.
33. *Mariners, Renegades and Castaways* (Detroit: Bewick/ED 1978).
34. *American Civilization*, p. 273f.

List of Thinkers Discussed in the Text

Alexander, Jeffrey C., sociologist (1947–)
Appiah, Anthony, social philosopher (1954–)
Arato, Andrew, sociologist (1944–)
Arendt, Hannah, political philosopher (1906–1975)
Barber, Benjamin, political scientist (1939–)
Benhabib, Seyla, political scientist (1950–)
Bercovitch, Sacvan, American literature (1933–)
Cohen, Jean, L., political theorist (1946–)
Crèvecoeur, Hector St John, farmer and writer (1735–1813)
Dahl, Robert A., political scientist, (1915–)
Dewey, John, philosopher (1859–1952)
Dworkin, Ronald, legal theorist (1931–)
Elshtain, Jean Bethke, political scientist (1941–)
Emerson, Ralph Waldo, philosopher (1803–1882)
Flacks, Richard, sociologist (1938–)
Gates, Henry Louis, literary critic (1950–)
Glazer, Nathan, sociologist (1923–)
Goldfarb, Jeffrey, C., sociologist (1949–)
Gutmann, Amy, philosopher (1949–)
Haartz, Louis, political scientist (1919–1968)
Hamilton, Alexander, politician (1757–1804)
Hirschman, Albert O., political economist (1915–)
Hofstadter, Richard, historian (1916–1970)
Holmes, Stephen, political scientist (1948–)
Isaac, Jeffrey C., political scientist (1957–)
James, C.L.R, social philosopher, literary critic and cricket expert (1901–1989)
James, William, psychologist (1842–1911)
Jay, John, attorney and politician (1757–1829)
Landes, Joan B., women's historian (1946–)
Lipset, Seymour Martin, political sociologist (1922–)
Madison, James, politician and former President of the US (1751–1836)
Mahan, Alfred Thayer, naval officer and historian (1840–1914)

Miller, Perry, historian (1908–1963)
Mills, C. Wright, sociologist (1916–1962)
Moore, Barrington Jr., sociologist (1913–)
Nozick, Robert A., philosopher (1938–)
Peirce, Charles Sanders, astronomer and philosopher (1839–1914)
Pocock, John G.A., intellectual historian (1924–)
Rawls, John, philosopher (1921–)
Rorty, Richard, philosopher (1931–)
Rosenblum, Nancy, political scientist (1947–)
Ryan, Mary P., women's historian (1945–)
Sandel, Michael J., political scientist (1953–)
Shklar, Judith N., political scientist (1928–1992)
Taylor, Charles, philosopher (1931–)
Thompson, Dennis, political philosopher (1940–)
Tocqueville, Alexis de, politician and writer (1805–1859)
Turner, Frederick Jackson, historian (1861–1932)
Veblen, Thorstein, economist (1857–1929)
Walzer, Michael, philosopher (1937–)
Weber, Max, sociologist (1864–1920)
West, Cornel, philosopher (1953–)
Wolfe, Alan, sociologist (1942–)
Wolff, Robert Paul, philosopher (1933–)
Wolin, Sheldon S., political scientist (1922–)
Young, James P., political scientist (1934–)

Annotated Bibliography

General

Of the many introductory texts that have been written, two accounts by prominent American intellectuals stand out: Charles Beard and Mary Beard: *The Rise of American Civilization* (New York: Macmillan Company 1930) and Max Lerner: *America as a Civilization* (New York: Henry Holt and Company 1957). Among collections that introduce students to central texts in American social and political thought David Hollinger and Charles Capper's *The American Intellectual Tradition* (New York/Oxford: Oxford University Press 1997, 2 vols) and Richard Wightman Fox and James T. Kloppenberg's *A Companion to American Thought* (Malden, MA/Oxford: Blackwell 1995) are useful. In terms of introductory texts that summarise and interpret the main sources of American social and political thought Michael Foley's *American Political Ideas* (Manchester/New York: Manchester University Press 1991) can be highly recommended. Earlier attempts, each with its own distinct emphasis, were: Vernon L. Parrington: *Main Currents in American Thought*, Vols 1–3 (New York: Harcourt Brace Jovanovich 1927, 1930), Henry Steel Commager: *The American Mind* (New Haven/London: Yale University Press 1950) and from the same author *The Empire of Reason – How Europe Imagined and America Realized the Enlightenment* (Garden City, NY: Anchor Press/Doubleday 1977), Perry Miller: *The Life of the Mind in America* (New York: Harcourt, Brace and World 1965), Harvey Wish: *Society and Thought in Modern America* (New York/London: Longman, Green and Company 1957), Stow Persons: *American Minds* (New York: Henry Holt and Company 1958), Alan Pendleton Grimes: *American Political Thought* (Holt, Rinehart, and Winston, New York 1960), Lewis Perry: *Intellectual Life in America* (New York/London: Franklin Watts 1984), and Donald S. Lutz: *A Preface to American Political Ideas* (Lawrence, KS: University Press of Kansas 1992). Historically more specific than these general accounts is the work of the historian Richard Hofstadter. His *The American Political Tradition* (New York: Alfred Knopf 1948), *Anti-Intellectualism in American Life* (New York: Alfred A. Knopf 1962) and *Social Darwinism in American Thought* (Philadelphia: University of Pennsylvania Press 1944) are now considered to be modern classics in the field of intellectual history. Other attempts to historicise and to treat the development of American thought in its proper social context are Henry F. May's *The Enlightenment in America* (Oxford/New York: Oxford University Press 1976), George Cotkin's *Reluctant Modernism: American Thought and Culture, 1880–1900* (New York: Twayne Publishers 1992), Laurence R. Veysey's *The Emergence of the American University* (Chicago/London: The University of Chicago Press 1965), Dorothy Ross' *The Origins of American Social Science* (Cambridge: Cambridge University Press 1991), Lewis A. Coser's: *Men of Ideas* (New York: The Free Press 1965), and from the same author *Refugee Scholars in America* (New Haven/London: Yale University Press 1984). Thomas Bender's *New York Intellect* (New York: Alfred A. Knopf 1987) and Alan M. Wald's history of *The New York Intellectuals* (Chapel Hill/London: The University of North Carolina Press 1987) are attempts to portray the intellectual life of the most vibrant and intellectually challenging American cities. If one wonders whatever happened to intellectual life after the great time of the New York intellectuals, one should read Norman Birnbaum's *The Politics of Ideas in Modern America* (New York: Pantheon Books 1988). No intellectual argument without its counterpart; thus anti-Americanism abroad and at home are the subject of James W. Ceasar's *Reconstructing America – The Symbol of America in Modern Thought* (New Haven/London: Yale University Press 1997), Richard Pells' *Not Like Us – How Europeans have loved, hated, and transformed American Culture since World War II* (New York: Basic Books 1997) and two studies by Paul Hollander: *Political Pilgrims* (Lanham, MD/London: University Press of America 1990) and *Anti-Americanism* (New York/Oxford: Oxford University Press 1992).

Many social and political ideas are not formulated and promoted in books but rather in journals and magazines. Amongst the mass of publications the following magazines and journals stand out; in alphabetical order they are: *American Journal of Sociology, American Journal of Political Science, American Political Science Review, American Quarterly, Cardozo Law Review, Commentary, Commonweal, Constellations, Critical Inquiry, Cultural Critique, Cultural Studies, Daedalus, Dissent, Ethics, Journal of Democracy, Partisan Review, Philosophy and Public Affairs, Political Science and Politics, Political Science Quarterly, Political Theory, Politics & Society, Publius, Social Forces, Social Problems, Studies in American Political Development, The American Historical Review, The American Journal of Legal History, The American Scholar, The Atlantic Monthly, The Nation, The New Republic; The New Yorker* and *The New York Review of Books.*

Exceptionalism

The first 'official' statement discussing exceptionalist American conditions is of course James Madison, Alexander Hamilton and John Jay: *The Federalist Papers*, first published in 1788 (London/New York: Penguin Books 1987). One of the most remarkable sources in terms of revealing the intellectual background of the Founding Fathers is *The Republic of Letters – The Correspondence between Jefferson and Madison* (New York/London: N.N. Norton and Company 1995). Benjamin Franklin's *Writings* (New York: The Library of America 1987) provides further hints concerning the intellectual background of the generation that proclaimed independence and founded the American republic. The historical, social and political contexts under which the Federalists wrote are described in Stanley Elking and Eric McKitrick's truly comprehensive study *The Age of Federalism* (New York/Oxford: Oxford University Press 1993). A pioneer and early forerunner of exceptionalism is Hector St John Crèvecoeur's *Letters from an American Farmer*, originally published in 1793 (Oxford/New York: Oxford University Press 1997). The exceptionalism thesis later became reformulated, most prominently by Frederick Jackson Turner in *The Frontier in American History* from 1920 (New York: Dover Publications 1996) and Alfred Thayer Mahan in *The Influence of Sea Power upon History*, first published in 1890 (New York: Dover Publications 1987). That America and its political foundations were less exceptionalist than anticipated but rather followed economic interests is the thesis of Charles A. Beard in *An Economic Interpretation of the Constitution of the United States* (New York/London: Macmillan/The Free Press 1913). All these contributions look at important aspects, yet remain somehow shallow when compared to the treatment of American exceptionalist conditions in Alexis de Tocqueville's classic *Democracy in America*, first published in 1835 (London: Fontana Press 1994). Tom Paine and Edmund Burke also discuss America's political uniqueness, although not under the heading 'exceptionalism', see *The Thomas Paine Reader* (ed. Isaac Kramnick and Michael Foot, London/New York: Penguin 1987) and Isaac Kramnick (ed.) *The Portable Edmund Burke* (New York: Penguin Putnam 1999). How the Tocquevillian thesis can be reformulated for twentieth-century conditions can be studied in the writings of Seymour Martin Lipset, particularly in *The First New Nation* (New York: Basic Books 1963), *Continental Divide* (New York/London: Routledge 1990) and *American Exceptionalism* (New York/London: Norton 1996). In comparison with Lipset, Hannah Arendt's discussion of exceptionalism in *On Revolution* (New York: Viking Press 1963) and in various of her *Essays in Understanding* (New York/San Diego: Harcourt Brace and Company 1994) is less sociologically grounded; Arendt instead stresses the importance of exceptionalism in the context of the rediscovery of 'the political'. Amongst the more modern approaches to American exceptionalism Byron E. Shafer (ed.): *Is America Different?* (Oxford: Clarendon Press 1991) is useful; the contributors to this volume not only look at social or political aspects, they also discuss the various economic and religious aspects of exceptionalism. One important aspect of the exceptionalism thesis is the discussion of Werner Sombart's question of *Why is There No Socialism in the United States?* (Originally published in German in 1906; an English translation appeared in London: Macmillan 1976.) Various students of American social history have tried to answer Sombart's thesis; amongsts the best are Paul Buhle: *Marxism in the USA* (London/New York: Verso 1987) Mike Davis: *Prisoners of the American Dream* (London/New York: Verso 1986), Kim Voss: *The Making of American Exceptionalism* (Ithaca/London: Cornell University Press 1993), and Irving Howe: *Socialism and America* (New York: Harcourt Brace Jovanovich 1977). Of course one can only say that something is exceptional when one compares and contrasts; Fredrick B. Pike's *The United States and Latin America – Myth and Stereotypes of Civilization and Nature* (Austin: University of Texas Press 1992) is a wonderful sourcebook for these purposes.

Political Theology

Amongst the many general accounts Sidney E. Ahlstrom's earlier attempt in *A Religious History of the American People* (New Haven/London: Yale University Press 1972) and Catherine L. Albanese's updated and somewhat more pluralistic account *America – Religion and Religions* (Belmont, CA: Wadsworth Publishing Company 1992) provide useful background reading. Compared to these studies, Ralph Barton Perry's *Puritanism and Democracy* (New York: The Vanguard Press 1944) is more specific in his attempt to describe the relationship between politics and religion. Perry Miller's work remains fundamental and unsurpassed, as can be seen particularly in his groundbreaking study *The New England Mind – From Colony to Province* (Cambridge, MA: The Belknap Press of Harvard University Press 1953) and in his collection of essays *Errand into the Wilderness* (Cambridge, MA: Harvard University Press 1956). Sacvan Bercovitch's study *The American Jeremiad* (Madison, WS: The University of Wisconsin Press 1978) and his essay collection *The Rites of Assent – Transformations in the Symbolic Construction of America* (New York/London: Routledge 1993) try to broaden aspects of the religiously founded Jeremiad first described by Miller. The same holds true for Michael Walzer's political interpretation of early religious thought in his two studies *The Revolution of the Saints* (Cambridge: Harvard University Press 1965) and *Exodus and Revolution* (New York: Basic Books 1985). The classic statement of the relationship between and further development of religious practice and belief and capitalist ideas can be found in Max Weber: Hans Gerth and C. Wright Mills (ed.) *From Max Weber: Essays in Sociology* (New York: Oxford University Press 1946). What the relationships between the various religious groups meant for the further development of America and what kind of political impact this had is discussed in Will Herberg's now classic study *Protestant, Catholic, Jew* (Garden City, New York: Anchor Books 1960). A more up-to-date discussion of the same aspects can be found in Peter W. Williams (ed.): *Perspectives on American Religion and Culture* (Maldon, MA/Oxford: Blackwell 1999). Religious developments and how they can lead to political fundamentalism are also subject to Garry Wills' fierce, yet informed critique *Under God – Religion and American Politics* (New York: Simon and Schuster 1990).

Republicanism

For a more general account of the history of republicanism Paul E. Rahe's *Republicanism Ancient and Modern* (Chapel Hill/London: University of North Carolina Press 1992), Gordon S. Wood: *The Creation of the American Republic, 1776–1787* (Chapel Hill: The University of North Carolina Press 1969) and from the same author *The Radicalism of the American Revolution* (New York: Alfred A. Knopf 1992), Isaac Kramnick's *Republicanism and Bourgeois Radicalism* (Ithaca and London: Cornell University Press 1990) and Joyce Appleby's: *Liberalism and Republicanism in the Historical Imagination* (Cambridge, MA: Harvard University Press 1992) are very helpful. John G.A. Pocock's work remains the classic statement in terms of intellectual history, especially in his study of *The Machiavellian Moment – Florentine Political Thought and the Atlantic Republican Tradition* (Princeton, NJ: Princeton University Press 1975). In two collections of essays *Politics, Language and Time: Essays in Political Thought and History* (New York: Athenaeum 1971) and *Virtue, Commerce and History: Essays on Political Thought, Chiefly in the Eighteenth Century* (Cambridge: Cambridge University Press 1985) Pocock has also tried to refine some aspects of his intellectual history of republican thought. Hannah Arendt's work, particularly her study *On Revolution* (New York: Viking Press 1963) is the attempt to revitalise the republican tradition, while Judith N. Shklar's *Ordinary Vices* (Cambridge, MA: The Belknap Press of Harvard University Press 1984) is the attempt to be more specific and to find out how particularly one central aspect of republican thought, virtue, can be conceptualised from a contemporary standpoint. The two posthumously published collections of Shklar's essays *Political Thought and Political Thinkers* (Chicago/London: The University of Chicago Press 1998) and *Redeeming American Political Thought* (Chicago/London: The University of Chicago Press 1998) also reveal the many-sided aspects of republican thought, particularly its relationship with liberal ideas. Michael Sandel's *Democracy's Discontent* (Cambridge, MA: The Belknap Press of Harvard University Press 1996) has been described as a modernised 'Fusion Republicanism'. Other aspects of Sandel's attempt to re-discover republican ideas are discussed in Anita L. Allen and Milton C. Regan Jr.: *Debating Democracy's Discontent* (Oxford/New York: Oxford University Press 1998).

Liberalism

The classic statement on the hegemony of liberal ideas in America is Louis Hartz's study *The Liberal Tradition in America* (New York: Harcourt Brace and World 1955). James P. Young's *American Liberalism* (Boulder, CO: Westview Press 1996) is the attempt to revise and elaborate on Hartz. Against a type of purely abstract reasoning concerned with liberalism's fate, Theodore J. Lowi's more empirically grounded study *The End of Liberalism* (New York/London: W.W. Norton and Company 1979) can add new factual dimensions to the discussion. Against comprehensive attempts John Rawls' *Political Liberalism* (New York: Columbia University Press 1993) is somehow 'minimalist' in its attempt to conceptualise American democracy and to provide it with a liberal philosophical foundation. Rawls' *Collected Papers* (Cambridge, MA: Harvard University Press 1999) provides additional material for the discussion. Judith N. Shklar's collection of essays *Political Thought and Political Thinkers* (Chicago/London: The University of Chicago Press 1998) and *Redeeming American Political Thought* (Chicago/London: The University of Chicago Press 1998) made clear that Shklar was also 'minimalist' in her approach to liberalism; yet her attempt to define the 'liberalism of fear' differs considerably from Rawls' – not least because of the attempt to conceptualise liberalism historically. Shklar's attempts remained not without admiration, as a posthumously published collection devoted to her work shows: Bernard Yack (ed.): *Liberalism without Illusions* (Chicago/London: The University of Chicago Press 1996). Stephen Holmes' *Passions and Constraints*

(Chicago: Chicago University Press 1995) resembles Shklar's efforts, but is somewhat more comprehensive. A study by the same author, *The Anatomy of Antiliberalism* (Cambridge, MA: Harvard University Press 1993), reveals the obstacles and some-times open hostility that liberalism has to confront, in both America and Europe. However, there have been sophisticated attempts to argue why liberalism is flawed or problematic. The classic statements are: Robert Paul Wolff: *The Poverty of Liberalism* (Boston: Beacon Press 1968), C.B. McPherson: *The Political Theory of Possessive Individualism* (Oxford: Clarendon Press 1962) and from the same author: *The Life and Times of Liberal Democracy* (Oxford: Oxford University Press 1977). Also to be recommended is the collection gathered by Michael L. Sandel (ed.): *Liberalism and its Critics* (New York: New York University Press 1984) and Dan Avnon and Avner de-Shalit (ed.): *Liberalism and its Practice* (London/New York: Routledge 1999). Contributors to these two volumes are not overtly hostile to liberal ideas, however they do see problems with its applications in the contemporary world.

Pragmatism

Pragmatism – A Contemporary Reader edited by Russel B. Goodman (New York/ London: Routledge 1995) gives a useful introduction and provides a representative selection of texts. An early forerunner to Pragmatism was Ralph Waldo Emerson, as can be seen in his *Writings* (New York: The Library of America 1983). Although Charles Sanders Peirce deserves the credit for having been the first pragmatist, it was *The Writings of William James*, edited by John J. McDermott (Chicago and London: The University of Chicago Press 1977) that made Pragmatism popular in the United States. With John Dewey, Pragmatism reached its zenith. Representative of Dewey's work are his *Reconstruction in Philosophy* (New York: Henry Holt and Company 1921/revised edition: Boston: Beacon Press 1948), an account of his philosophy, together with his liberal coda voiced in the political pamphlet *The Public and its Problems* (New York: Henry Holt and Company 1927). After John Dewey and George Herbert Mead, Pragmatism became more concrete in its analysis and could thus demonstrate the relevance of its social criticism. Thorstein Veblen and C. Wright Mills became the chief promoters of pragmatist ideas. *The Portable Veblen*, edited by Max Lerner (New York: Viking Press 1948) collects the best work of Veblen; as does a collection of essays written by C. Wright Mills and edited by Irving Louis Horowitz: *Power, Politics and People* (New York: Oxford University Press 1963). Today Richard Rorty has taken on the role of being the most prominent representative of Pragmatism. In his *Contingency, Irony, and Solidarity* (Cambridge: Cambridge University Press 1989) and in various essays, published as *Philosophical Papers* (3 vols; Cambridge: Cambridge University Press 1991 and 1998), he has tried to spell out what Pragmatism means these days. There is now also a growing list of literature that tries to see Pragmatism in its proper historical, social and political contexts. See for example Cornel West's *The American Evasion of Philosophy – A Genealogy of Pragmatism* (Madison, WI: The University of Wisconsin Press 1989), H.O. Mounce's *The Two Pragmatisms* (London/New York: Routledge 1997), and

Hans Joas' *Pragmatism and Social Theory* (Chicago: University of Chicago Press 1995). For more specific accounts see George Cotkin's *William James, Public Philosopher* (Baltimore: Johns Hopkins University Press 1990), John Westbrook's *John Dewey and American Democracy* (Ithaca/London: Cornell University Press 1991) and Hans Joas' *G.H. Mead – A Contemporary Re-examination of his Thought* (Cambridge: Polity Press 1985).

Democracy and Power

The classic study of how and why democracy developed in the Western world is Barrington Moore's *Social Origins of Dictatorship and Democracy* (Boston: Beacon Press 1966). Moore's findings are further discussed in Theda Skocpol's *States and Social Revolutions*, (Cambridge: Cambridge University Press 1988) and Theda Skocpol (ed.) *Social Revolutions in the Modern World*, (Cambridge: Cambridge University Press 1996). In terms of what happened after democracy had finally been established, C. Wright Mills' trilogy consisting of *The New Men of Power* (New York: Harcourt, Brace and Company 1948); *White Collar* (Oxford/New York: Oxford University Press 1951) and *The Power Elite* (Oxford/New York: Oxford University Press 1956) is still provocative reading, particularly in terms of how the relationship between democracy and power structures is been perceived. G. William Domhoff and Hoyt B. Ballard's (ed.) *C. Wright Mills and the Power Elite* (Boston: Beacon Press 1968) collects various responses to Mills. One of the most prominent challengers of Mills was the political scientist Robert A. Dahl. *A Preface to Democratic Theory* (Chicago/London: The University of Chicago Press 1956), *Who Governs?* (New Haven/London: Yale University Press 1961), *Democracy and its Critics* (New Haven/London: Yale University Press 1989) and finally *On Democracy* (New Haven/London: Yale University Press 1998) belong to the finest literature dealing with the state modern American democracy is in. Since Mills and Dahl defined the goalposts, various attempts have been made to update and/or modify the analysis of democracy. Amongst these many attempts are: Joshua Cohen and Joel Rogers: *On Democracy* (New York: Penguin 1983), Adam Przeworski: *Capitalism and Social Democracy* (Cambridge: Cambridge University Press 1985) and Samuel Bowles and Herbert Gintis: *Democracy and Capitalism* (New York: Basic Books 1986). The most recent approach to understanding and explaining modern democracy is that of 'deliberative democracy'. Amy Gutmann and Dennis Thompson's *Democracy and Disagreement* (Cambridge, MA: The Belknap Press of Harvard University Press 1996) stands out in this respect and is probably the most ambitious attempt so far. A forerunner in thinking about 'deliberative democracy' has been Benjamin Barber. *Strong Democracy* (Berkeley/Los Angeles: University of California Press 1984) and a collection of his essays *A Passion for Democracy* (Princeton, NJ: Princeton University Press 1998) are proof of that. How heterogeneous the 'deliberative democracy' approach is can be seen in two collections: Jon Elster (ed.): *Deliberative Democracy* (Cambridge: Cambridge University Press 1998) and Seyla Benhabib (ed.): *Democracy and Difference* (Princeton, NJ: Princeton University Press 1996).

Justice and Injustice

John Rawls' work *A Theory of Justice* (Cambridge, MA: Harvard University Press 1971) must now be considered one of the greatest philosophical works of political philosophy in modern times. In his *Collected Papers* (Cambridge MA: Harvard University Press 1999) Rawls gives further hints for the interpretation of this work. Robert A. Nozick sympathises with the idea of a revival of political philosophy yet is highly critical when it comes to Rawls' theory. In *Anarchy, State, Utopia* (Oxford: Blackwell 1975) he raises some serious questions concerning Rawls' *Theory of Justice*. The same holds true for Robert Paul Wolff. Wolff argues not from a libertarian neoliberal background (as does Nozick) but from a Marxist perspective. *Understanding Rawls* (Princeton, NJ: Princeton University Press 1977) is one of the best accounts, if not the best, for students attempting to understand Rawls' work. Michael Walzer's *Spheres of Justice* (New York: Basic Books 1983) argues against a one-dimensional conception of justice, while Barrington Moore's *Injustice – The Social Bases of Obedience and Revolt* (New York: M.E. Sharpe 1978) and his *Reflections on the Causes of Human Misery* (Boston: Beacon Press 1969) must be seen as attempts to concretise the question of justice by looking at concrete historical examples and specific social and political circumstances. Judith N. Shklar also has a deeper sense of such concrete circumstances. Additionally, as can be seen in her studies *Faces of Injustice* (New Haven/London: Yale University Press 1990) and *American Citizenship* (Cambridge, MA: Harvard University Press 1991), Shklar not only has a clear understanding but also a vision for the future in terms of the complex relationship and interaction between social and political rights. The 'language of rights' has also been a concern to Ronald Dworkin. His *Taking Rights Seriously* (Cambridge, MA: Harvard University Press 1978) is a must. Various other dimensions that stem from a conception of justice in a liberal context are discussed in Michael J. Sandel: *Liberalism and the Limits of Justice* (Cambridge: Cambridge University Press 1982), Bruce Ackerman: *Social Justice in the Liberal State* (New Haven: Yale University Press 1980) and Stephen Holmes and Cass R. Sunstein: *The Cost of Rights* (New York: W.W. Norton and Company 1999). A general overview of the history of American constitutionalism provides Michael Les Benedict: *The Blessings of Liberty* (Lexington, MA: D.C. Heath and Company 1996).

Pluralism and Multiculturalism

One of the best sourcebooks on the subject of pluralism and multiculturalism is Stephen Thernstrom (ed.): *Harvard Encyclopedia of American Ethnic Groups* (Cambridge, MA: The Belknap Press of Harvard University Press 1980); not only does it contain the history of every imaginable ethnic group, it also contains relevant thematic essays, from 'assimilation' to 'immigration policies' to 'pluralism'. Out of the many texts on multiculturalism Daniel J. Elazar's *The American Mosaic* (Boulder/ San Francisco: Westview Press 1994) stands out as a thorough attempt to conceptualise America's complex cultural landscape. Ronald Takaki's (ed.) *From*

Different Shores (New York/Oxford: Oxford University Press 1994) and David Theo Goldberg's (ed.) *Multiculturalism – A Critical Reader* (Oxford/Cambridge, MA: Blackwell 1994) are readers which collect and introduce students to the most important writings on multiculturalism. The same holds true for Ellen Card Du Bois and Vicky L. Ruiz's reader (ed.) *Unequal Sisters – A Multicultural Reader* (New York/London: Routledge 1990) – except that the focus is on gender issues. What it meant to fight for civil rights becomes clear when one studies the historical documents and speeches: Clayborne Carson's et al. (ed.) *The Eyes on the Prize Civil Rights Reader* (New York: Viking Penguin 1991) is probably the best compendium available. Another compendium, edited by John K. Roth, *American Diversity, American Identity* (New York: Henry Holt and Company 1995) provides the reader with information on how multiculturalism and pluralism also found its expression in American literature. It was W.E.B. Du Bois who said that one of the most important problems to be solved in the twentieth-century is the problem of the colour line. *W.E.B. Du Bois – A Reader*, edited by David Levering Lewis (New York: Henry Holt and Company 1995), collects and introduces the pioneering writings of the man himself. A few decades after Du Bois, multiculturalism has entered the mainstream of social and political thought with Charles Taylor's reflections on *Multiculturalism and 'The Politics of Recognition'* (Princeton, NJ: Princeton University Press 1992), Michael Walzer's *What it means to be an American* (New York: Marsilio 1992) and *On Toleration* (New Haven/London: Yale University Press 1997) from the same author, and K. Anthony Appiah and Amy Gutmann's *Color Conscious* (Princeton, NJ: Princeton University Press 1996). Very much in the spirit of W.E.B. Du Bois but less philosophically compared to Appiah and Gutmann are Henry Louis Gates' *Loose Canons – Notes on Cultural Wars* (New York/Oxford: Oxford University Press 1992), Cornel West's *Race Matters* (Boston: Beacon Press, 1993) and a collaborative effort of Henry Louis Gates and Cornel West *The Future of the Race* (New York: Alfred A. Knopf 1996). Bell Hooks' *Killing Rage: Ending Racism* (London/New York: Penguin 1996) is a collection of essays that looks particularly at the relationship between gender and race. Albert Murray's *The Omni-Americans* (New York: Outerbridge and Diestfrey 1970) and *The Collected Essays of Ralph Ellison* (ed. Saul Bellow; New York: The Modern Library 1995) were very much written in the spirit of a universalist ethos (without neglecting the particularistic roots of African-American culture) – a combination one rarely finds these days. The same is true for the collection edited by Robert G. O'Meally: *The Jazz Cadence of American Culture* (New York: Columbia University Press 1998). In recent years the sometimes all too particularistic talk of multiculturalists has come under fire; Todd Gitlin's *The Twilight of Common Dreams* (New York: Metropolitan Books 1995), Arthur Schlesinger's: *The Disuniting of America* (New York: W.W. Norton and Company 1991), Nathan Glazer's *We are all Multiculturalists Now* (Cambridge, MA: Harvard University Press 1997) together with Richard Rorty's *Achieving Our Country* (Cambridge, MA: Harvard University Press 1998) belong to the more self-reflexive critiques. The various pros and cons of multiculturalism are also discussed in Avery F. Gordon and Christopher Newfield (ed.): *Mapping Multiculturalism* (Minneapolis/London: University of Minnesota Press 1996) and Paul Berman (ed.): *Debating P.C.* (New York: Dell Publishing 1992). An attempt to raise the level of the discussion on multiculturalism and pluralism with the help of the 'civil society' concept has been made by the various contributors in Jeffrey C. Alexander (ed.): *Real Civil Societies* (London/Thousand Oaks, CA: Sage 1998). Appreciative but more sceptical about the practical application of the civil society concept is Adam B. Seligman: *The Idea of Civil Society* (New York: Free Press 1992).

Civil Society, Social Theory and the Task of Intellectuals

Throughout the century leading intellectuals have made suggestions on how the relationship between social theory, civil society and the task of intellectuals should be perceived. Some of the finest examples of such writings are Robert S. Lynd: *Knowledge for what?* (Princeton NJ: Princeton University Press 1939), C. Wright Mills: *The Sociological Imagination* (New York/London: Oxford University Press 1959), from the same author the collection *Power, Politics and People* (New York/London: Oxford University Press 1963), Daniel Bell: *The End of Ideology* (New York: The Free Press 1962) Robert K. Merton: *Social Theory and Social Structure* (New York: The Free Press 1957) and Russel Jacoby: *The Last Intellectuals* (New York: Basic Books 1987). Richard Flacks' *Making History* (New York: Columbia University Press 1988) is the attempt to take stock, that is, to theorise about both failures and achievements of the past. Also the conservative and neoliberal approaches and their attempt to take stock should not be ignored: Irving Kristol: *Two Cheers for Capitalism* (New York: Basic Books 1972) and Norman Podhoretz *Making It* (New York: Random House 1967) are representative of the spirit of the times. *The Essential Neoconservative Reader*, edited by Mark Gerson (Reading, MA: Addison-Wesley Publishing 1996), provides a handy, representative sample of neoconservative writings that are otherwise not so easily traceable and accessible. Good background reading is George H. Nash: *The Conservative Intellectual Movement in America since 1945* (New York: Basic Books 1976). An attempt to mediate between the somewhat conservative search for values and the community and the rather liberal approach to politics and civil rights is communitarianism. The communitarians' celebrated book then was Robert Bellah et al.: *Habits of the Heart. Individualism and Commitment in American Life* (Berkeley/Los Angeles: University of California Press 1985). A new representative collection of the movement is Amitai Etzioni (ed.): *The Essential Communitarian Reader* (Lanham, MD: Rowman and Littlefield 1998). However, after 1989 the world looks different and American intellectuals have reflected on that change. The most ambitious attempts in this respect are Jean L. Cohen and Andrew Arato: *Civil Society and Political Theory* (Cambridge, MA: MIT Press 1992), Jeffrey C. Isaac: *Democracy in Dark Times* (Ithaca/London: Cornell University Press 1998), Jeffrey C. Goldfarb's trilogy: *On Cultural Freedom* (Chicago/London: The University of Chicago Press 1982), *The Cynical Society* (Chicago/London: The University of Chicago Press 1991) and *Civility and Subversion* (Cambridge: Cambridge University Press 1998), Sheldon S. Wolin: *The Presence of the Past*

(Baltimore/London: The Johns Hopkins University Press 1989) and Richard Rorty: *Contingency, Irony, and Solidarity* (Cambridge: Cambridge University Press 1989). Some of the best contributions in the attempt to rethink the link between social theory, civil society and the task of intellectuals have come from feminists. Jean Bethke Elshtain's *Public Man, Private Woman* (Princeton, NJ: Princeton University Press 1981) is a prime example. How varied and internally pluralistic feminist views are these days can be seen in the contributions to two Oxford readers which collect the main texts in the field: Anne Phillips (ed.): *Feminism and Politics* (Oxford/New York: Oxford University Press 1998) and Joan B. Landes (ed.): *Feminism, the Public and the Private* (Oxford/New York: Oxford University Press 1998).

Social and Political Thought at the Dawn of the Twenty-first Century

At the end of the twentieth century attempts have been made to revive public philosophy in America. The most prominent example is Michael J. Sandel's *Democracy's Discontent* (Cambridge, MA: The Belknap Press of Harvard University Press 1996). The wide response Sandel's work triggered is gathered in Anita L. Allen and Milton C. Regan Jr.: *Debating Democracy's Discontent* (Oxford/New York: Oxford University Press 1998). That the state of civil society is better than intellectual republicans think it is is the argument in Nancy L. Rosenblum's Tocquevillean argument in *Membership and Morals: The Public Use of Pluralism in America* (Princeton, NJ: Princeton University Press 1998). Very different from these studies are attempts that try to 'trespass' academic boundaries and disciplines like those of Albert O. Hirschman: *Exit, Voice, and Loyalty* (Cambridge, MA: Harvard University Press 1970), *The Passions and the Interests: Political Arguments for Capitalism before its Triumph* (Princeton, NJ: Princeton University Press 1977), *Shifting Involvements: Private Interests and Public Action* (Princeton, NJ: Princeton University Press 1982) and *The Rhetoric of Reaction* (Cambridge, MA: The Belknap Press of Harvard University Press 1991). Alan Wolfe is another name that comes to mind when talking about 'trespassing' of academic boundaries and envisioning a new 'human science' for the twenty-first century: *Whose Keeper? Social Science and Moral Obligation* (Berkeley/Los Angeles: University of California Press 1989). Of course there can be no vision of the future of a new 'human science' without reflecting on the role intellectuals have to play. In this respect Michael Walzer's work has been a pioneering effort, see particularly his *Interpretation and Social Criticism* (Cambridge: Harvard University Press 1987) and *The Company of Critics* (New York: Basic Books 1988). How far intellectuals' love for their country can go can be seen in a collection of essays that were provoked by a statement from Martha Nussbaum (ed. Joshua Cohen): *For Love of Country – Debating the Limits of Patriotism* (Boston: Beacon Press 1996). In this context it is sometimes healthy to be reminded of some old-fashioned internationalism, particularly when it is seen in the light of American experiences, as was the case with C.L.R. James. Particularly recommended should be his *American Civilization* (London/New York: Routledge 1996) and *Mariners, Renegades and*

Castaways (Detroit: Bewick/ED 1978), an almost unknown work which deserves a wider readership since it is one of the most informed pieces ever written about America. Lastly, it is always helpful to find out what people from outside think about one's own country. In this respect the view of another American, the Brazilian Alfredo G.A. Valladao's account *The Twenty-First Century will be American* (London/ New York: Verso 1996) could prove to be extremely helpful.

Glossary

Agnosticism, agnostic: A belief that questions whether the ultimate cause and the essential nature of things can be known; refers to uncertainty of ultimate knowledge.

Agrarian society, industrialised society: A distinction that many social scientists have come to use since it was first 'invented' by political economy and later radicalised in Karl Marx's critique. Both adjectives 'agrarian' and 'industrialised' refer to the dominant mode of production, agriculture or industry. The transition from feudalism to capitalism is crucial to the clear definition of both.

American Civil War: The War of Succession between eleven seceding Southern states ('the South') and the United States Government, 'the North' (1861–1865). The war resulted in the abolition of slavery.

American Revolution: The events (1776–1787) that started out with the Declaration of Independence and that finally, after a long war with Great Britain, led to the formation of the American Republic. The American Revolution can be interpreted as both the first modern anti-colonial conflict and as a social revolution.

Ancien régime: The antiquated regime or ruling class that desperately tries to hang on to power and to prevent radical change from happening. The term was first coined to identify the ruling circles that tried to prevent the French Revolution.

Anti-Americanism: A prejudice, attitude or opinion that is opposed to anything American, regardless of its quality or benefit.

Anti-Intellectualism: An attitude directed against intellectual efforts and thinkers. American anti-intellectualism has strong populist, that is democratic, roots.

Aristocracy: The stratum of society in which all individuals belonging to that class are of inherited privilege and rank.

Assimilation, difference, hyphenated nationalities: The merging of cultural traits from previously distinct cultural groups. In the course of American history cultural groups have also claimed the right to be accepted on the basis of their cultural, political or social difference. The general framework of the United States usually allows space for both claims, hence the concept of hyphenated nationalities (Italian-American for example) in which the individual can decide on which side of the hyphen he/she wants to be.

Bill of Rights: The first ten amendments of the American Constitution listing those rights that every citizen has against the state or government.

Bourgeoisie: The property-owning citizens, according to Karl Marx the class that manages to turn the economic power of capitalist wealth into political capital.

Branches of Government: Most modern democracies introduced a model that separated yet also maintained the links between the legislative, executive and judiciary branch. This was introduced to prevent the concentration of powers – but also with the intention of making pluralist forms work.

Calvinism: The name refers to John Calvin, a Swiss religious activist. Calvinism is particularly strong in terms of its defence of predestination and the sovereignty of God; it is anticipated that salvation comes only through hard work and rigidly regulated forms of life.

Capitalist spirit, entrepreneurial spirit: The German sociologist Max Weber first coined this term. It refers to Protestant values such as hard work and disciplined behaviour – in short, a work ethic that allows capitalist ideas to thrive. This spirit was particularly important in the early phase of modern capitalism.

Charismatic leadership: A term first used by Max Weber referring to the capacity of outstanding, powerful, charismatic individuals to influence the modern political and bureaucratic process.

Checks and balances: Limits imposed on the three branches of government (legislative, executive and judicial) to prevent the accumulation of power.

Citizen, citizenship: The idea of citizenship goes back to ancient Greece and Rome. In modern times it refers to the formal criteria of being a member of nation-state; in substantial terms it means to have civil, political and social rights. The relationship between rights and privileges and the duties of citizens remains, to this day, an important topic of debate.

Civic associations: Sometimes also referred to as voluntary associations. The existence of multiple social, political, economical or cultural organisations that form the backbone of modern civil society.

Civic humanism: A system or mode of civic thought or action in which human concerns are of primary importance. This term is often used in classic and modern republican thought.

Civil religion: A secularised form of beliefs and actions pertaining to democratic and civil arrangements.

Civil rights: The fundamental rights of free citizens that no state or government can take away, occasionally also referred to as a part of human rights (together with political rights). Most of the civil rights legislation in the United States goes back to the amendments of the United States Constitution.

Civil society: First conceived of by such thinkers as John Locke, Adam Ferguson and Hegel, the first modern notion of civil society incorporated all actions and activities of associations and social groups that were not directly linked to the state. Marx later denounced this concept as serving to mask powerful, influential property and market relations. Recently the concept of civil society has seen a revival, first in Eastern and Central Europe where the concept of civil society was used against the all-powerful communist state and helped to develop a parallel society opposed to the communist regimes; later the concept of civil society also became a strong conceptual tool for Western social scientists in search of renewed activities in a complacent Western society – a society that (despite all the criticism) also provided the tools for its own renewal.

Colonialism: Following the demise of their Spanish and Portuguese predecessors, the most prominent and 'successful' colonial empires were the British Empire and its French counterpart. The aim of colonialism changed and differed over time. Whereas one of the missions of the British was 'to export civilisation' (including its law tradition), French colonialism, in contrast, never aimed at such high purposes. However, one of the first blows that the British Empire received was the establishment and independence of the American Republic, the 'First New Nation'. In the later decolonisation process, America played a major anti-colonial role (a role that would not prevent America from pursuing imperialist interests at a later stage).

Committee on Public Safety: The leading force in a particularly violent period during the French Revolution.

Communitarianism: A movement that rejects the extreme selfish individualism that it sees as prevalent in contemporary society; communitarianism puts the emphasis on strengthening community-related activities and relations and thus aims at reviving modern civil society. The movement itself is very hetero-geneous and includes such thinkers as Amitai Etzioni, Michael Walzer and Charles Taylor.

Congress: Congress is the legislative branch of government in the United States. It consists of two chambers, the House of Representatives and the Senate. The House of Representatives consists of members who are elected on the basis of population (determined by a regular census), and are elected for two years. The Senate represents the interests of the states, regardless of the size and population of the states (each state elects and sends two senators, the period is five years).

Conspicuous consumption: A term coined by Thorstein Veblen to denounce the consumption of the affluent American leisure class.

Conspiracy, conspirational ideas: The idea that a few selected powerful individuals have the means to influence major historical events by secretly planning and co-ordinating their political activities.

Constitution, constitutionalism: In contrast to its British counterpart, the American judicial system, based on the Constitution, the Bill of Rights, the interpretation of the Federalist Papers and the various rulings of the Supreme Court, has always presented liberty in more positive terms, thus inventing a 'rhetoric of rights' and developing a 'rights culture' around the primary documents and texts.

Contract theory, social contract: The idea of a social contract has biblical roots and first entailed a contract between God and the Chosen People. The English philosopher Thomas Hobbes was the first to present the social contract in more secularised terms, as a contract between a monarch and the people, whereby the king granted security and the people delivered obedience – the entire enterprise leading to stable order. John Locke conceived of the social contract in more liberal terms whereby the people delegated their sovereignty to a ruler and in exchange were granted a certain minimum of security and liberty, the difference to Hobbes being that the monarch was granted sovereignty only in limited terms, that is if the monarch failed to 'deliver', the people had the right to withdraw their support.

Cultural apparatus: A term used by C. Wright Mills to refer to the growing stratum of intellectuals in modern institutions that deal mainly with symbols, that is the media, higher education etc.

Deism: Deists believe in a supreme being without necessarily following or practising any particular religious doctrine. Most of the Founding Fathers were influenced by Enlightenment philosophers and their emphasis on reason; consequently they disregarded the practice of organised religion at the time. Deists are not equivalent to atheists; in their majority deists respect the idea of a higher supreme being that created the world but that has remained somehow indifferent to its further development.

Deliberation, deliberative democracy: The purposeful, reflective use of democratic means and ends.

Democracy, Madisonian democracy, populist democracy, hybrid model of democracy, capitalist democracy, participatory democracy: Literally democracy means the rule of the people; originally a practice in classical Athens, democracy was later re-invented and re-formulated under modern conditions. While Madisonian democracy paints a realistic picture of the pluralistic forms in modern democracy in that it accepts representation and the formation of a ruling elite as long as it remains accountable to the people, populist democracy aims at a more radical conception and criticises the drift of decision-making processes away from the people. Over two centuries America has learned to come to terms with both the pros and cons of the two models, developing a 'hybrid model of democracy'. Capitalist democracy is just another term for such a hybrid model. Participatory democracy demands more than the acceptance of the status quo and requires the active involvement of citizens in the decision-making processes that have an impact on their life.

Despotism, despotic government: The exercise of absolute authority; the opposite of democratic government in that it is arbitrary, non-rational, non-legitimated, and non-accountable.

Determinism, structural determinism: An interpretation that sees the world and social events as being completely determined by structural forces, independent of individual human beings or human will or effort.

Dictatorship: The rule and power of one or more people opposed to any democratic decision-making procedures.

Differentiation, fine distinctions: Emile Durkheim was the first sociologist to explain the modern differentiation process by hinting at the more complex and interdependent forms in modern society. Standing in the classic tradition, Pierre

Bourdieu has made the most recent effort to explain an even further differentiation process by looking at fine distinctions such as food consumption patterns, education, cultural credentials, and so on.

Earning and voting: Mutually related terms first introduced by Judith N. Shklar to emphasise the distinction and the complex relationship between political and social rights.

Elite, power elite and mass society: C. Wright Mills was the first sociologist to conceive of American society and its political process in terms of a small tripartite elite (consisting of the economic, political and military elite) that made history (in a perversion of Marx's concept of making history more democratic) in that it made all the important decision – thus creating an apathetic mass society.

Empire(s): An aggregate of nations and peoples, held together by a supreme sovereign power (historically a king, emperor or other powerful statesman) on a territory that is much larger than the size of the modern nation-state.

English Civil War: The conflict (1642–46) between English Parliamentarians and Royalists.

Epistemology, epistemological paradigm, epistemological democracy: Epistemology investigates the origins, nature and methods and limits of human knowledge; an epistemological paradigm uses a certain example or an entire set of examples to illustrate its central argument. Epistemological democracy makes the attempt to democratise human knowledge by introducing concepts that help to advance the democratic cause.

Equality and achievement: Being politically equal and having the same rights, American citizens have always been opposed to the European idea of absolute equality in terms of social conditions and preferred the idea of achieving equality of opportunity through such means as education.

Errand: A journey to convey a message or for a specific purpose; occasionally errand can refer to the purpose of the journey itself.

Eschatology: A theological doctrine that is concerned with final or last matters.

Ethnicity, voluntary character of ethnicity: A social group or a subpopulation of individuals that share historical, organisational, cultural characteristics and/or religious belief systems. Ethnicity or aspects of it can be ascribed (from non-members or majority populations) or voluntarily exposed (in terms of self-segregation).

Exceptionalism: The theory that regards America as different from European societies. Alexis de Tocqueville was the first one to write about the exceptionalist American conditions in his *Democracy in America*. A more contemporary approach is that of the political sociologist Seymour Martin Lipset (who sees himself as standing in the Tocquevillean tradition).

Exit, voice and loyalty: Terms used by the economist Albert O. Hirschman. Exit refers to the leaving option while voice stands for the option of speaking out or protest; loyalty encourages or often enables voice and keeps exit at bay.

Exodus: A metaphor that interprets later events of immigration or departure in the light of the early experiences of the people of Israel in their flight from Egypt (as described in the Old Testament).

Federalism, Federal Government: Pertaining to the nature of a union of states under a central, federal government; it is distinct from the government of these states.

Feudalism: Holding of land for a fee; feudalism refers to the social and economic order in which feudal ideas prevail. In contrast to Europe, North America never knew any feudal structures.

First Amendment: The First Amendment to the Constitution of the United States grants freedom of religion, free speech and freedom of association.

First New Nation: A term first introduced by the political sociologist Seymour Martin Lipset, referring to the fact that America was the first colony to break away from a European motherland. It was also the first nation to have had a successful revolution and to establish a political process that made the United States the first and oldest modern democracy.

Founding Fathers, Framers of the Constitution: The first generation of American revolutionaries who signed the Declaration of Independence, fought in the War of Independence, drafted the Constitution and influenced the early political formation of the American Republic.

French Revolution: The events (1789–1799) that overturned the *ancien régime* of the French Crown and Aristocracy. The French Revolution became significant for the rest of the world, because it was the first collective effort in Europe to demand liberty, equality and fraternity, thus inspiring their inheritors to pursue the unfulfilled dreams of the French Revolution. The Russian Revolution (1917) was the most radical effort in this respect.

Frontier, Frontier thesis: A theory which gained academic credibility through the historian Frederick Jackson Turner; the approach criticises the notion that the United States were mainly formed by and influenced through the early experiences of New England.

Gilded Age: The golden age of unregulated economic growth and enterprise ('Robber Barons'), following the time of the Civil War and Reconstruction. Mark Twain brought popularity to the term.

Glorious Revolution: Another expression for the the political events in England (1688–89), that allowed the whiggish elements of society to become more influential.

Hegemony, cultural hegemony: Predominant influence, not necessarily political and social. The Italian Marxist Antonio Gramsci hinted at the possibility and chances of gaining cultural hegemony and power (as opposed to pursuing the Leninist path of gaining solely political power).

Hermeneutics, hermeneutic: The art of interpretation. The concept of Greek origins was later used for theological and historical purposes. (The German theologist Schleiermacher was one of the pioneers of hermeneutics). It was also used to distinguish the activities of the social sciences from those of the natural sciences. Its most prominent representatives are Dilthey, Max Weber, Hans-Georg Gadamer and Jürgen Habermas.

History-making: A term used by proponents of participatory democracy. History-making refers to the right and the actual capacity to have a say in the decisions that have an impact on one's life.

Hommes de lettres: Another expression for those pro-Enlightenment intellectuals who criticised and opposed the French *ancien régime*.

Homo faber, homo politicus: A distinction that plays a major role in classic and modern political philosophy. Homo faber is the working or producing man who, because he is working or producing, is limited to the realm of necessities (he has to transform nature in one way or another). In contrast, the homo politicus is free from such 'ballast' or burden of dealing with necessities and nature and operates in the 'realm of freedom'. The crucial distinction here is between means and ends. The homo faber remains means-centred (he is bound by the possibilities or limitations of nature), whereas the homo politicus is ends-oriented (and is free to deal with other human beings, normally as ends in themselves, for example in the political arena).

Human geography: An approach that conceives of human action and political events in terms of a specific location in space. The Frontier thesis can be regarded as a human geography approach.

Individualism: A modern concept first introduced by Alexis de Tocqueville in his *Democracy in America*, marking the difference between traditional societies (in which the group, clan, caste or class plays an important role) and modern societies (in which the individual and individual responsibility are more important).

Inequality, complex spheres of inequality: It was only with the French Revolution and the discovery that man can indeed make history and that every person was free in principle and had the right to be treated equally that the question of social class and social stratification entered the collective consciousness. With the rise of industrial capitalism the question of equality and inequality became even more urgent. While Marx's theory knows only two classes that are directly related to each other (one lives from the surplus production of the other), Max Weber talks about class and social inequality in terms of a continuum (to be determined by the position the individual occupies in the market). Michael Walzer conceives of complexity in modern societies such as the United States in terms of non-transcendable spheres, each with its own complex structure.

Jacksonian Democracy: An age of further democratisation (initiated and promoted by so-called Jacksonians, that is admirers and supporters of President Andrew Jackson). The Jacksonian Age is usually considered to be the period following the early years of the establishment of the American Republic.

Jeremiad: Originally a lamentation or mournful complaint, the Jeremiad has become a rhetorical device or tool to interpret and explain a variety of occurring events in the light of theological scriptures; it was most commonly used by Puritan settlers.

Justice as fairness, distributive justice, well-ordered society: Terms first coined by the philosopher John Rawls to conceptualise his *Theory of Justice*. In order to achieve justice, a society has to operate on the basis of fair procedures; furthermore it has to use distributive mechanisms to achieve or to establish fairness as a procedural means; both preconditions lead to the assumption that only a well-ordered society can become a just society.

Laissez-faire capitalism, state intervention, Keynesianism: Laissez-faire symbolises an attitude that can be described as 'letting the people do as they choose', and is an early idea of political economists to promote free trade and a self-regulating market. State intervention only became necessary after the experience of the world economic crisis in 1929, an event that demonstrated that the absolutely unregulated market can have disastrous results. Keynesianism (referring to the ideas of the British economist John Meynard Keynes) promoted state intervention and initiatives to prevent the market from collapsing again. In the United States these initiatives became known as part of the New Deal.

Liberalism, economic and political liberalism, liberalism of fear, procedural model: A set of loosely defined doctrines that hold that it is the purpose of the state and society to enable individuals to pursue their own fortune and maximise the capacity of individuals to make choices in order to achieve maximum happiness. While economic liberalism puts more emphasis on a free market (with minimum state interference), political liberalism aims at securing the political rights that would enable citizens to achieve these aims. The term 'liberalism of fear' was first coined by the American political scientist Judith N. Shklar to make clear that American political liberalism was a latecomer in that it responded mainly to European atrocities of the twentieth century. Liberalism has been accused by Republican thinkers of being only a procedural model, that is 'empty' in terms of its own purposes and ends. Opposed to the idea of only procedural (means-oriented) ideas, republicans have suggested the idea of a formative (ends-oriented) republic.

Liberty, positive and negative liberties and rights, libertarian ideas: One of the central themes in Enlightenment philosophy and one of the most important demands in the French Revolution. Theorists differ in terms of stressing the importance of a negative or positive conception of rights and liberties. While European, and particularly English, law stresses the negative dimension, the American tradition emphasises the positive aspects. It is important to stress that both libertarian and liberal thinkers agree that liberty is of intrinsic value; however they might disagree on the different means to achieve this aim.

Mercantile capitalism: A capitalism based on trade and commerce, a form of capitalism that does not play a major role in Marx's critique of political economy and is rather of Weberian origin in its conceptualisation.

Modernity, modern: A term that was made popular by the French poet Charles Beaudelaire to distinguish the new times from remote times or the old regime. The concept can not only distinguish modern times from the ancient or medieval times but can also refer to the 'here and now'. Modern society is usually regarded as a Western concept: to westernise is to modernise. However, the concept of modernity is a fuzzy concept with no clear-cut edges. In recent decades there has been a lively debate on what distinguishes the modern from the postmodern condition.

Monarchy, hereditary monarchy: A political system in which the power actually or nominally lies with the monarch; the power of the monarch is usually inherited.

Muckraking, Muckrakers: Journalists, critics and activists in the Gilded Age who criticised passionately the widespread corruption and scandals of American politics at the time.

Multiculturalism, E pluribus unum: The idea of a pluralism of ethnic groups. E pluribus unum means 'out of many – one'.

Neo-liberals, neo-conservatism: A loose set of ideas that became prominent in the early 1970s, mainly as a response to the radical ideas of the 1960s. Most of the neoliberals supported the liberal agenda of civil and political rights, yet were opposed to state intervention or Keynesianist ideas in the economy. The more value-oriented, conservative forces later turned into neo-conservatists, supporting the Reagan administration and its tough stand during the Cold War.

New Jerusalem: A metaphor that has biblical roots, referring to the hope of rebuilding Jerusalem in the New World. Since the first settlers were Puritans with a good knowledge of the Old Testament it was just a short step to apply the biblical idea to the new circumstances.

New middle class: A term first coined by the American sociologist C. Wright Mills. The new middle class can be distinguished from the old middle class. The old middle class consisted mainly of independent shopkeepers, small entrepreneurs, craftsmen and independent farmers. In contrast, almost all the new middle class jobs are with larger corporations where there is much more dependency within a clearly defined hierarchy.

Normativity, normative structures: Values, patterns of behaviour, questions of morals. Normative structures are well-established patterns that consciously or unconsciously underlie social action of individuals or social groups. Also, social and political theories are not value-free and might have hidden values.

North, South: Two regions in the United States representing two different forms of civilisation – one based on modern capitalist production, the other one on the political economy of slavery. The American Civil War ended the conflict on slavery, yet many cultural traits in the South remained unchanged, even after a period of Reconstruction.

Old World, New World: Usually Americans referred to Europe as the Old World, while Europeans referred to America as the New World. The distinction is not limited to geographical coordinates, but also refers to cultural, political and social distinctions.

Original position, public reasoning, overlapping consensus: Terms introduced by the political philosopher John Rawls to conceptualise his *Theory of Justice* and his idea of *Political Liberalism*. While the original position functions as a modern substitute for the old state-of-nature debate (as theorised by the natural law tradition in philosophy), the existence of public reasoning must be understood as a precondition for the proper functioning of any liberal society; the same applies to the overall and commonly accepted idea of functioning political principles (the 'overlapping consensus').

Parliamentary democracy: Democratic arrangement in which the parliament plays the major role and is at the heart of the decision-making process.

Party of Hope, Party of Memory: Terms first used by the political scientist Judith N. Shklar to explain the main differences within the American political tradition. While the Party of Hope emphasises the new beginning and the new dawn of the American republic, the Party of Memory stresses that the mistakes of the past should not be forgotten.

Philadelphia Convention: The Convention that came together in Philadelphia to discuss new political arrangements after the American War of Independence. The Convention ended with the proposal for the American Constitution and actually led to the founding of the American Republic.

Pluralism: A normative perspective that emphasises the existence and competition of a plurality of political, social and economic groups in modern society. Usually pluralism accepts the probability of conflict and demands mutual tolerance.

Political culture: A system of beliefs, symbols, and values that has an impact on political action in a particular nation-state, region, or ethnic group.

Political economy: A term 'invented' in the late eighteenth century, referring to measures of the government to influence or regulate trade, exchange, money and taxes. Its most prominent representatives came from the Scottish Enlightenment: Adam Smith, Sir James Steuart, and David Ricardo. Later political economy was criticised (most prominently by Karl Marx) for forgetting the social exploitative dimension of modern economic relationships.

Political equality: Ideally citizens should be treated equally, not according to their social standing, rank, or class. In the American context the idea of political equality and political rights have been used as a means to achieve social equality.

Political Science: The academic discipline that tries to understand and explain the role of politics in modern society. Political science has developed into various sub-disciplines or branches, that is political theory, political history, comparative politics, international relations and so on. Some of the American Founding Fathers, in particular Alexander Hamilton, James Madison, John Jay, and Thomas Jefferson together with the French observer Alexis de Tocqueville, are now regarded as the first modern political scientists.

Political Sociology: An academic sub-discipline that looks at the social bases of politics.

Political Theology: A term theorised by the German legal theorist Carl Schmitt to emphasise that all modern political conceptualisations derive from theological thought and have religious origins – and are therefore nothing but secularised theological concepts.

Pragmatism: An American philosophical approach that criticises and rejects big system-like theory and the essentialism that can be found in most of European philosophy. It is common to distinguish between two pragmatisms: the first that occurred at the turn of the century, led by Charles Sanders Peirce, William James and John Dewey, and a second, more contemporary, approach, represented most prominently by Hilary Putnam and Richard Rorty.

Protestant work ethic: A term first coined by the sociologist Max Weber to describe the cultural roots of early modern capitalism (based on an entrepreneurial spirit and hard work).

Public philosophy: The openly discussed and promoted *raison d'etre*, or a public commitment of a nation or a nation-state to a particular cause.

Public and private sphere: A distinction crucial for the understanding of modern civil society. The idea of the private sphere has traditionally been linked to the household, to personal relationships and family relations, but also to the idea of economic activities. In contrast, the term 'public sphere' refers to all activities outside these previously mentioned activities: public institutions such as parliaments, universities, theatres, publishing activities and so on. Both concepts are understood as 'fuzzy concepts' meaning their distinction is useful but not very 'sharp'. There is an ongoing debate in the social sciences on which activities are to be considered private and which are public (work and other 'economic' activities are just two examples).

Puritans, Puritan ideas: The first settlers who came to America and settled down in New England had left England because they felt that their religious ideas were not fully respected and accepted by the Church of England. Additionally, in a country where only one form of religious practice was tolerated, religious conflict often took on the form of political dissent. It is thus not by accident that in Puritan ideas and practice, theology and political ideas became entwined.

Rational and legitimate forms of power and coercion: Terms first coined by the sociologist Max Weber to describe democratically acceptable forms of political coercion and power.

Rechtsstaat, Sozialstaat: German expressions and concepts that indicate the task or purpose of a state or government. A *Rechtsstaat* is a state in which the rule of law is of primary importance. The *Sozialstaat* is a state that guarantees that citizens have minimal social security (usually in order to avoid social and political conflict and in order to have equality of opportunity). A *Rechtsstaat* does not necessarily have to be a *Sozialstaat*, while the modern *Sozialstaat* is usually a *Rechtsstaat*.

Reformation: The reform movement, which criticised the then all-powerful Catholic Church, and the decisions that were made in Rome at the time. The main regions and countries in which the Reformation became either the dominant force or had at least some success were Switzerland, Germany, the Netherlands, Britain and Scandinavia.

Republicanism, republican ideas: Amongst republican ideas it is useful to distinguish between classic and modern, European and American forms. The classic examples of republicanism and republican thought are Rome and the

Italian city states. More modern examples are the American and French Republic. The ideas of virtue or virtuous action are central to republican thought, be it classic or modern. Republican ideas had to change in order to fit new conditions – hence the distinction between American and European forms of republicanism.

Restoration: Usually refers to periods after a revolution, where parts of the pre-revolutionary conditions are re-established (mainly because the Revolution went too far, was too radical, or too innovative).

Rights, ideas of rights, rhetoric of rights, natural rights, inalienable rights: John Locke was the first one to conceptualise rights as belonging to nature, hence their inalienable character and the term 'natural rights'. Rights are conceived of as being either specific (as due to one specific person or group) or universal (everyone can claim it and/or has to respect it). Furthermore, the distinction between positive rights (as enabling rights) or negative rights (as constraints) is crucial. The American constitutionalist tradition represents the former, while the English tradition represents the latter – hence the emphasis in America on the rhetoric of rights.

Rule of law: The rule of principles guided by law, usually a constitution, or a set of acceptable norms. Under the rule of law every citizen is regarded as equal.

Russian Revolution: The popular February Revolution (1917) against the Czarist regime and the so-called October Revolution of the same year in which the Bolsheviks gained power from the earlier established provisional government.

Salvation: The idea of deliverance from the power and penalty of sin played a major role in Protestant thought. Hard work was usually seen as a precondition for a life without sin, thus anticipating possible salvation.

Sects: The United States recognises no state church. Although America is known as the most religious country in the Western world, the religious practice is mostly exercised in religious sects and a plurality of churches. It is assumed that in the past the plurality of religious Protestant sects helped to develop the acceptance and tolerance of political pluralism – eventually leading to the peaceful co-existence of various social groups.

Secular: wordly, profane (as opposed to 'religious' and 'holy').

Separation of Powers: A system of diverting and channelling political interests for the purpose of the common good of the democratic process.

Social Darwinism: The application of Darwinist ideas to social and economic life. In the United States Social Darwinism was not infrequently promoted by sociologists.

Socratic figure: A person who lives or is committed to the idea that the unexamined life is not worth living.

Sovereignty of the Parliament, Sovereignty of the People: In the British constitutional tradition absolute emphasis is given to the Parliament (the British system for example has no equivalent to the American Supreme Court), while the American political system is based on the notion of the Sovereignty of the People. Accordingly, the American political system distributes power more democratically.

System, lifeworld, colonisation: Analytical distinctions coined by the contemporary German social philosopher Jürgen Habermas. System refers to those realms of social, political and economic life where strategic and instrumental action prevails. In contrast, the lifeworld is the sphere in which non-instrumental, communicative action is dominant. In Habermas' theory, the system relies on the resources of the lifeworld in order to function – however, in the real world, instrumental and strategic action seem to become the dominant forms, that is the system colonises the lifeworld.

Terror, terreur: During the course of the French Revolution a radicalisation process occurred. The Committee on Public Safety established a regime of terror in which individuals who were considered to be opposing the revolution were persecuted, arrested, and often guillotined. Since the Russian revolutionaries saw themselves as fulfilling the 'unfinished business' of the French Revolution, it was not by chance that terror and widespread atrocities also became genuine features of the Russian Revolution.

Third Estate: The poorest yet largest stratum of pre-revolutionary France, hence the equating of *le peuple* (the people) with the Third Estate. It was supposed that the *Sansculottes*, the more radical elements of *le peuple*, together with the *hommes de lettres* (writers, lawyers, advocates, the lower stratum of the state employees) were the main forces behind the radicalisation process of the French Revolution.

Totalitarianism: A label used to identify political and social systems in which a powerful directorate (a leader, a party, or both) attempts to control all aspects of life. A crucial aspect of totalitarian society is the abolishment of the distinction between private and public life. Further radicalisation in a totalitarian country may lead to terror and mass destruction. Both National Socialism and Stalinism are considered to have been totalitarian systems.

Tyranny of the majority: A term first coined by the French nobleman Alexis de Tocqueville. The term denounces the conformity that can result from a political process that is genuinely based on political equality aspects of a given democratic system. The danger that Tocqueville foresaw in particular was that a democratically elected legitimate majority could form a government that imposes its will on a minority.

Universalism, particularism: A doctrine that knows no exceptions; a set of ideas that can be universally applied (human rights for example). Particularism refers to the exact opposite, that is to something that stands out, is special or peculiar.

Utilitarian ideas: The doctrine assumes that the achievement of individual happiness stems from the conscious decision of individuals and that virtue is ultimately based on utility. Its compromised ideal is the greatest happiness of the greatest number of people.

Virtue, corruption: Concepts that play a major role in both classic and modern republican thought. While virtue is essential for maintaining the *res publica,* corruption is its anticipated death.

Volonté general: The general will, sometimes also referred to as the people's will.

Index